SEMANTICS IN BIBLICAL RESEARCH

STUDIES IN BIBLICAL THEOLOGY

A series of monographs designed to provide clergy and laymen with the best work in biblical scholarship both in this country and abroad

STUDIES IN BIBLICAL THEOLOGY

Second Series · 24

SEMANTICS IN BIBLICAL RESEARCH

New Methods of Defining Hebrew Words for Salvation

JOHN F. A. SAWYER

ALEC R. ALLENSON INC.
635 EAST OGDEN AVENUE
NAPERVILLE, ILL.

ISBN 0-8401-3074-0
Library of Congress Catalog Card No. 72-75901

Published by Alec R. Allenson Inc.
Naperville, Ill.
Printed in Great Britain

This book is dedicated to the memory of

SHLOMO GRODZENSKY

(1905-1972)

לעליית נשמתו

CONTENTS

PREFACE

This book is the revised version of a thesis submitted to the Faculty of Divinity in the University of Edinburgh in 1968 under the title 'Language about Salvation. An analysis of part of the Vocabulary of the Old Testament'. For my enthusiasm for Old Testament research in general I am enormously indebted, like a host of other students, to my supervisor, Professor Norman W. Porteous, who introduced me to the Old Testament in the first place and has been a source of inspiration in many ways ever since. While I have limited myself here mainly to linguistic matters, there are several points, especially in Chapter II, 'Context', and Chapter III, 'Semantic Fields', at which the study might have gone, at the instigation of Professor Porteous, in a more theological direction, and to which it is hoped one day to return. For guidance and stimulation during my years as a postgraduate student, I am scarcely less indebted to Dr John C.L. Gibson, whose meticulous criticisms and numerous constructive comments at every stage were invaluable.

Of the many others whose instruction, advice or encouragement I hope I have nowhere unwittingly abused, I must mention two by name: Dr Hans Kosmala, whose famous 'round-table' seminars in the library of the Swedish Theological Institute, Jerusalem, provided unique experience in handling texts, not only biblical, but also talmudic and sectarian, and Professor Chaim Rabin, whose pioneering course in semantics at the Hebrew University in 1963 was for many of us the beginning of a new era in the study of the language of the Old Testament.

Finally I should like to thank John Pellowe of the Department of English Language in the University of Newcastle upon Tyne for casting an eye, perhaps more charitable than critical, over the finished product before it left my hands, and my mother for her characteristically immaculate proof-reading and indexing. My thanks are also due to Mrs Ternant, part-time secretary in the Department of Religious Studies, and I gratefully acknowledge assistance from the University's generous Research Fund.

Newcastle upon Tyne J.F.A.S.
March 1972

ABBREVIATIONS AND SYMBOLS

ANET	*Ancient Near Eastern Texts relating to the Old Testament*, ed. J. Pritchard, 2nd ed., Princeton, 1955
ASTI	*Annual of the Swedish Theological Institute in Jerusalem*, Leiden
ATD	Das Alte Testament Deutsch, Göttingen
AV	Authorized Version of the Bible, 1611
BASOR	*Bulletin of the American Schools of Oriental Research*, New Haven, Conn.
BDB	F. Brown, S.R. Driver and C.A. Briggs, *A Hebrew and English Lexicon of the Old Testament*, Oxford University Press 1907
BH^3	*Biblia Hebraica*, ed. R. Kittel, 3rd ed., Stuttgart 1937
BKAT	Biblischer Kommentar. Altes Testament, Neukirchen-Vluyn
BL	H. Bauer and P. Leander, *Historiche Grammatik der hebräischen Sprache*, Halle 1922
BSOAS	*Bulletin of the School of Oriental and African Studies*, London
BZAW	Beihefte zur *Zeitschrift für die Alttestamentliche Wissenschaft* (Giessen) Berlin
DLZ	*Deutsche Literaturzeitung*
EVV	English versions of the Bible
ExpT	*Expository Times*, Edinburgh
GK	*Gesenius' Hebrew Grammar*, ed. E. Kautzsch, 2nd English ed. by A.E. Cowley, Oxford University Press 1910

HAT	Handbuch zum Alten Testament, Tübingen
ICC	International Critical Commentary, Edinburgh
JB	The Jerusalem Bible, Darton, Longman and Todd 1966
JBL	*Journal of Biblical Literature,* New York, New Haven, Philadelphia
JNES	*Journal of Near Eastern Studies,* Chicago
JSS	*Journal of Semitic Studies,* Manchester
KB	L. Koehler and W. Baumgartner, *Lexicon in Veteris Testamenti Libros,* Leiden 1953; *Supplementum,* 1958
LXX	*Septuaginta*
MT	Masoretic text
NEB	The New English Bible, with Apocrypha, Oxford University Press 1970
NP	Noun-phrase
NT	New Testament
OT	Old Testament
OTL	Old Testament Library, SCM Press
PEQ	*Palestine Exploration Quarterly,* London
RSV	The Revised Standard Version of the Bible, 1952
SBT	Studies in Biblical Theology, SCM Press
SVT	*Supplements to Vetus Testamentum,* Leiden
TDNT	*Theological Dictionary of the New Testament.* English translation of *TWNT* by G.W. Bromiley, Grand Rapids, Michigan, 1964ff.
TGUOS	*Transactions of the Glasgow University Oriental Society*
TWNT	*Theologisches Wörterbuch zum Neuen Testament,* ed. G. Kittel and G. Friedrich, Stuttgart 1933ff.
V	Verb
VT	*Vetus Testamentum,* Leiden
ZAW	*Zeitschrift für die Alttestamentliche Wissenschaft* (Giessen) Berlin

Symbols

*	'reconstructed form' (see p. 93)
>	'develops historically into'
+	concatenation (see pp. 63, 79)
CAPITALS	lexeme
underlined	transcription from particular context

I

INTRODUCTION

It may seem odd that, after so many centuries of lexicography, translation and exegesis, the meaning of several common Hebrew terms can still be the subject of a monograph. In biblical research, however, such a study is not by any means unusual. In recent years there have been many lengthy word- or root-studies,[1] and the reasons for this state of affairs are also reasons why it is hoped that the present study is not going to be entirely superfluous.

Since 1961, when Barr's *Semantics* sent a 'wind of change' through modern biblical criticism,[2] semantics has been a fashionable and controversial subject, introduced into, or at least referred to in the majority of studies in biblical language and theology.[3] The discussion has, however, tended to be so preoccupied with criticism of faulty linguistics and with methodology and underlying presuppositions that common sense and the practical experience of handling semantic problems have often been to a greater or lesser extent neglected.[4] There have been a few studies in which experiments in the use of 'semantic fields' have been presented;[5] there has been some discussion of verbal and non-verbal context;[6] and in addition to these more or less self-conscious attempts to improve semantic theory, there have been several studies in which modern semantic theory (although not under that name) is already implicit.[7]

But none of these recent essays in semantics has taken as its prime aim the systematic isolation and solution of all the practical semantic problems that arise in this area of biblical research. The present attempt to do this, in the context of a description of several Hebrew terms for salvation, is thus intended to be at the same time a study in theory and in practice. New theory is introduced only when it has some immediate practical advantages, and, alongside some of the more important insights of modern linguistics, common sense and practical convenience are constantly aimed at. New or unnecessarily opaque terminology is avoided wherever possible: where perfectly intelligible terms like 'meaning' are available, for example, these are used freely, on the assumption that wherever they occur, they are limited enough by their context to preclude any ambiguity or vagueness. Arbitrary decisions have been consciously taken at many stages in the argument in order to limit the terms of reference and make for maximum precision rather than completeness. This means, incidentally, that subjects dear to the hearts of some linguists and OT scholars, and which they would not conceive of a semantic study omitting, are perhaps left out. Only aspects of semantic theory that were found in practice to be essential have been examined, and what started out as an analysis of several biblical terms became, as it were, a practical guide to describing the meaning of OT Hebrew.

In the field of biblical research, semanticists – and this may include philologists, lexicographers, exegetes and theologians – have a distinct advantage over their colleagues in other branches of linguistics in having a closed literary corpus to work with. The first step in any semantic work is to define this corpus precisely: does this corpus consist of a reconstructed 'original' (unpointed) text, or the masoretic text? A decision is required right at the beginning if precision and consistency are to be achieved. There follows the question of historical context: what is the situation (or non-verbal context) in which the text has meaning? As there are clearly many possible answers to this question, another decision must be made to examine the meaning of the text as it is understood in a particular, carefully defined situational context. Maximum objectivity is again the aim, and the essential distinction between synchronic and historical description underlined. Within OT Hebrew there are varieties of language and because the meaning of a term may vary from one to another, distinctions must be drawn in terms of style or literary form. Again the terms of reference are narrowed and a particular style selected as the verbal context of the terms to be described (Chapter II).

One way to define a term is to distinguish it from terms semantically related to it, and this can best be done by reference to the semantic field to which the term belongs. In the centre of the large associative field of HOŠIA‘, a lexical group consisting of eight terms is isolated, and these are the terms to be described in detail. Within the associative field, some interesting information on the semantic structure of some of the terms is also examined (Chapter III). The synchronic analysis, in which various modern theories are applied to the task of describing the meaning of the terms as they are used in the context already defined (Chapter IV), is followed by a brief historical description of the terms and etymologically related terms against the wider background of the Hamito-Semitic family (Chapter V). The problem of presenting semantic information in the form of convenient definitions is tackled (Chapter VI), and finally some tentative general semantic principles are formalized (Chapter VII).

> Hoc quam non temere & cupide, sed peditentim & explorato, id quod rei gravitas jubebat, confirmarim, uno alterove exemplo palam facere fert animus; ubi quod illustrius ac luculentius in medium proferam vix habeo quam ea radix ex qua sibi Dominus *Jesus* nomen sumsit. (A. Schultens, *Origines Hebraeae,* Leiden, 1761)

II

CONTEXT

A definition of the word yešaʿ 'salvation', as it is understood in modern Europe, would no doubt begin with a reference to Arabic wasiʿa 'to be spacious'. Mowinckel, for example, defined yešaʿ as 'literally "wideness, spaciousness", i.e. favourable conditions, both in external political relationships, and in internal social, moral and religious conditions'.[1] Similar definitions have appeared regularly since 1761 when the Dutch scholar Albert Schultens published his theory that Hebrew *yšʿ was etymologically related to Arabic wasiʿa 'to be spacious'.[2] Whether or not the modern popular etymology is historically correct, it has inspired a beautiful definition of yešaʿ as it is understood today, and therefore an important stage in the semantic history of the word. This is 'what yešaʿ means' in the context of some modern lexicographical, exegetical and homiletical literature.

Presumably, for Schultens, Gesenius, Pedersen, Mowinckel and many others, the Gibeonites' call for help wᵉhošiʿa lanu wᵉʿozrenu 'Save us and help us!' (Josh. 10.6) is literally about *Lebensraum* and the relief of a besieged city, and the Psalmist's affirmation of faith ʾadam ubᵉhema tošiaʿ YHWH 'Man and beast thou savest, O Lord' is about the spaciousness and freedom that is God's gift to those whom he loves.

But as soon as we ask whether this is how the words were understood before 1761, or in ancient Israel, we have begun to distinguish various historical contexts in which the words 'have meaning'. The prehistory of the words can be extended back before their earliest Hebrew context to Ur (*c.* 2000 BC), Mari (eighteenth century BC) and Ugarit (fourteenth century BC), and their later history in Jerusalem, Alexandria, Qumran, Pumbeditha and so on from about the tenth century BC to modern times.[3] There is clearly a bewildering variety of historical contexts in which terms like HOŠIAʿ 'to save', YEŠAʿ 'salvation' and personal names like Hosea, Isaiah and Jesus have had meaning. Before we can hope to define the meaning of any of these terms, we have to define the historical contexts in which they have been understood.

To put this another way, we are not concerned, in defining meaning, only with what the original author meant, but also with how his original audience or readers understood him; and if we allow this, then we must also grant that the interpretations of later readers (who may or may not have discovered the author's original meaning) have as much claim on our attention as his original audience. Over and over again, ambiguity and vagueness can be overcome when this basic consideration is introduced. An example from the book of Amos will make this clearer.

What does w^{e}helilu širot hekal in Amos 8.3 mean? It seems likely that w^{e}helilu šarot hekal 'the palace singing-girls will wail' is what Amos actually said, and that he was addressing this judgment oracle to the high-living royal establishment at Samaria.[4] The reasons for the change to širot hekal in masoretic tradition would then be straightforward: hekal in Jerusalem denoted 'temple' rather than 'palace', particularly when the city was rebuilt after the exile with a temple much more prominent than a palace, and while there may have been širot 'songs' in the temple, there were certainly no šarot 'singing-girls'. For masoretic tradition, followed by AV and RSV, the *original meaning* of these words, as they were understood in Samaria in the eighth century BC, would have been of purely academic interest, whereas the words as they stand are addressed to Jerusalem and foretell the destruction of the temple in 587 BC, a central event in the history of Israel. If two historical contexts can be separated in this way, then ambiguity is removed. There is no need to say that hekal denotes either 'palace' or 'temple', as RSV and JB do: it denoted 'palace' in Samaria, but 'temple' after the oracle had been applied to Jerusalem. The decision on what it means today depends on arbitrary considerations: the NEB translators, for instance, have selected the original meaning of the term as it was used in Samaria in Amos' day, rejecting out of hand the later Jerusalemite development in the history of the phrase (one wonders whether, for consistency, the Davidic conclusion to the book of Amos should not also have been rejected as not being 'original'); the RSV, on the other hand, has given priority to the Jerusalemite interpretation of the phrase, which fits better into the historical context of the book of Amos as it stands now in the Jewish canon (and not in the Samaritan), but has retained the ambiguity by adding 'or palace' in a footnote. A prior decision on whether to translate passages, wherever possible, as they were understood originally, each in its own separate historical context, or as they have come down to us in the finished texture of complete books, would simplify the task of the translator immensely, and remove many inconsistencies and ambiguities. The first stage in semantic description is a precise definition of the historical situation or situations in which the words to be described are 'contextualized'.[5]

1. *Contextualization*

The pioneer in this field of contextualization, under the hardly less cumbersome term *Gattungsgeschichte,* was of course Hermann Gunkel.[6] His deceptively simple thesis was that every literary form *(Gattung)* was appropriate to its situational context *(Sitz im Leben)* in the social, cultural and religious life of ancient Israel. From the beginning this promised to be a fruitful line of research in OT studies for two main reasons. In the first place, there is a peculiarly wide variety of literary forms within the OT – political speeches, letters, legal documents, parables, love-songs, war-songs, laments, coronation hymns and the rest; and in the second place, at the beginning of the century a vast amount of new evidence was coming to light on almost every sphere of human activity in the ancient Near East, and Gunkel's methods of classifying it, by dividing it up into identifiable situations, were timely. His emphasis on the close relation between language and situation, and his realization that statements about the meaning of biblical language are only valid when they are statements about biblical language contextualized (thirty years, incidentally, before Malinowski and Firth)[7] eventually became the key to most modern OT interpretation.

The importance of Gunkel's methods for semantic theory cannot be overestimated. But there is one area in which he and many of his successors in the field of biblical criticism must be held responsible for a misleading emphasis. As we have already seen, the original *Sitz im Leben* of biblical language, however fascinating and academically rewarding a subject for research, is not the only situational context in which it has meaning. Most of the form-critical research of biblical scholars, particularly in the first half of this century, was exclusively concerned with the original situations in which the material was produced, and it is really only in recent years that later historical contexts, such as the historical context of the final form of the text and of textual 'corruptions', have been examined with the same enthusiasm as the original *Sitz im Leben* of each separate unit. The omission of the psalm-headings from the NEB, partly because 'they are almost certainly not original',[8] is a throwback to the days when originality was some guarantee of historical importance or authenticity. Even if the psalm-headings, in their present form, belong to the age of the Chronicler, let us say, about the fourth century BC, they are no less authentic than the book of Chronicles itself.[9] Timeless compositions like the psalms have been contextualized in many situations from the time they were first composed, which may actually have been before they were adapted for use in Israelite worship, right down to modern times.

The same is to some extent true of any piece of literature, and we might quote the example of Halliday's description of the language of a Chinese literary work, *The Secret History of the Mongols,* for which he finds it necessary to distinguish eight 'events in which the text operates'.[10] Many more than eight 'events' could be listed in which the OT is contextualized, and although this will obviously increase the semanticist's terms of reference, no biblical semantics would be complete without taking into account this wider notion of contextualization.

The first objection to this approach is likely to be that it gives *carte blanche* to all kinds of abuses. Where would one draw the line separating what a passage means from what it undoubtedly does not mean? Where would one fix the 'limits of interpretation'?[11] The form-critics seemed at first to provide the answer: by concentrating exclusively on the original situation and rejecting later contextualizations as unauthentic, it had become possible to discover what actually happened or what a prophet actually said. Not only has this proved to be overoptimistic, but a change of emphasis in biblical research, to which reference has already been made, has generated a new interest in the history of tradition, that is, in all the various ways in which a text has been understood, not only in one of them.

In an important monograph, *Isaiah and the Assyrian Crisis,* B.S. Childs analyses a historical process in which one event, which we shall never be able to reconstruct in detail, has evoked at least six distinct responses, each traceable to its own particular historical context: the prophetic oracles of Isaiah, the annalistic type report, the Deuteronomic redaction of historical tradition, the legend of the righteous king, the Chronicler's midrash, and the prophetic, eschatological liturgy.[12] The question he raises is whether one of these six different accounts of the Assyrian crisis is more authentic than the others. Childs asserts that biblical critics must make value judgments on varying elements in, for example, parallel texts, although he would reject some of the usual theological norms (historical accuracy, chronological priority), introducing instead the context of the early church. In other words, Childs is saying that if the biblical critic is to evaluate diversities in the OT, he is forced out of the context of OT research into a religious community in which arbitrary decisions, like those concerning the canon of scripture, are made for him to accept or reject. In so doing he is no longer acting as a detached exegete, but as a committed member of a religious community.[13]

Childs was dealing with the problem of the context of a number of passages relating to one historical event: the same kind of conclusions would apply to the context of smaller linguistic units, in particular, to individual words. When faced with a variety of definitions or interpretations of a particular word, for example, ʿabdi 'my servant' in Isa. 52.13, we are forced to step out of a 'discernment situation', to use Bishop Ramsey's language, into a 'commitment situation' if we want a single definition of what the word means.[14] Before reaching this 'moment of decision', however, there are plenty of useful statements on the meaning of biblical language which we can make, provided the historical context selected for each statement is carefully defined first. The meaning of OT traditions can be legitimately and rewardingly analysed on the basis of several, at times conflicting, but usually illuminating historical contexts in which they have been read and understood. Some of the fantastic interpretations of the early church fathers, for example, based on allegory and the like, are just as important for a complete description of the meaning of the text as the NT interpretations or those of the early Jewish rabbis. One may not agree with them, but this is not part of linguistic description. The writings of the Qumran sect, the Karaites, the Scottish Covenanters, the Seventh Day Adventists, the form-critics and the present writer all constitute contextualizations of OT words and passages, and all are therefore possible starting-points for semantic definition. 'No stage in this work's long period of growth is really obsolete', wrote Gerhard von Rad in a rather different context;[15] but it is interesting how closely this corresponds to the methods of modern linguists, who describe what is there without passing value-judgments.[16]

To return at last to the meaning of the word yešaʿ: the modern 'etymologizing' definition with which we began, namely, that yešaʿ 'literally means spaciousness', is as interesting and important as any other definition, provided its historical context is first defined and clearly distinguished from a pre-1761 context for which the same kind of evidence is so far entirely lacking.[17] What is quite inadmissible, and the deserving target of so much criticism since Barr's *Semantics*, is the assumption that because a word has a particular meaning in one context, it automatically has the same meaning in another quite different context a couple of thousand years earlier.

Many of our biblical commentaries take into account several contextualizations without making any clear attempt to keep them distinct. The masoretic text usually provides the starting-point; the 'original' meaning of the passage (whatever that means) is generally assumed to be the goal; the meaning of the passage in the NT is often included; and its meaning for us today or for the author himself is often interwoven with the rest. It is in fact frequently quite difficult to find an answer to the question 'What does this passage mean?' Naturally, subjective elements come into the discussion, and the commentator may select one or other of the meanings as the right one or the most important or the most relevant or the most illuminating. Very frequently the result of this selection is equated with the 'original' meaning in its 'original' context, and where this is not accessible to modern scholarship, the question of meaning is left open. We have seen, in the example from Amos above, how this semantic ambiguity can be avoided by substituting for the question 'What does it mean?' the questions 'What did it mean in its original context?' or 'What did it mean in Babylon in the sixth century BC?' or 'What did it mean in Alexandria in the third century BC?' and so on. Each question is different and may yield a different answer, but each is quite precise, each can be approached with exactly the same objectivity, and each belongs to the subject matter of the semantics of biblical language.

Every biblical passage is not equally well attested in the same historical contexts; and in any case commentators have their own interests in one or other of them, an archaeologist in the original one, a Christian in the Christian ones, a Jew in the Jewish ones, and each will inevitably select his own special emphasis. The essential thing is that he should make clear at the outset exactly what he is doing, since, in biblical research, semantic statements are not only about what a speaker meant, but also about what his hearers thought or believed he meant, and who the hearers in question are must be carefully defined.[18]

2. *Situational Context*

In the light of these remarks on the contextualization of biblical language, it will have become clear that for a definition of yešaʿ and the other Hebrew words for salvation to be adequate it must be preceded by a precise account of the context or contexts in which the terms were uttered and understood. In the present study one of the situational contexts in which the terms have been contextualized is selected, and all subsequent statements on their meaning apply only to how they were understood in that context. It must be emphasised that the present writer is well aware that this is only one of the many legitimate levels at which it is possible to conduct a semantic analysis of biblical language. But the advantages of thus fixing exact terms of reference at the beginning will become evident at every stage, and this arbitrary decision is merely intended to ensure precision and objectivity, while at the same time stressing the need for this preliminary stage in all types of semantic description, from lexicography to exegesis and biblical theology.

For present purposes, then, it has been decided that the final form of the text as preserved in masoretic tradition and transmitted to us in the Codex Leningradensis, should be the literary corpus in which the terms to be discussed occur, and that how the masoretes themselves understood the text should be the subject for semantic analysis. At first sight this will appear to be identical with the position adopted by the fundamentalist, both Christian and Jewish. The difference, however, lies in the awareness already referred to, that this is a quite arbitrary decision and that research at other levels of interpretation, including that of the original historical context in ancient Israel, is equally legitimate and often more rewarding. The fundamentalist believes that the level selected by himself, whatever it may be, has unique, divine authority; whereas the present approach is based on purely practical, methodological considerations. The reasons for the present choice of context, although in the last resort it must be admitted this choice is an arbitrary and subjective one, can be set forth as follows.

1. The final form of the text is still often neglected in commentaries and translations. Martin Noth, for example, while recognizing the need to study the final form, is clearly more interested in the separate threads (e.g. J, E, D, P) than in the finished texture:

> In its present state the book is as it were a fabric, skilfully woven from a series of threads, and the only satisfactory way of analysing a fabric is to keep firmly in sight the threads of which it is made up and the material of which the threads themselves are composed.[19]

In the words 'the only satisfactory way', Noth comes close to an uncompromising position dangerously like that of the fundamentalist. The NEB's omission of the Psalm-headings because they are 'almost certainly not original' (while retaining the book of Daniel which is even later) shows a similar ambivalent attitude to what biblical scholarship is concerned with.[20] The persistent division of the book of Isaiah into three parts is not only historically confusing (parts of 'Proto-Isaiah' are later than parts of 'Trito-Isaiah'), but also detrimental to the study of certain important 'Isaianic' themes and concepts.[21] Or perhaps it might be admitted that the printing of Isaiah 1-39 as a separate book is mainly for practical reasons.

The absence of any serious discussion of the final form of the text in many works is due to a number of factors in modern scholarship: the continuing novelty of the discoveries of the last hundred years which have thrown such a flood of fascinating light on the ancient Near East (witness the steady flow of books on biblical archaeology); the subsequent reaction away from the conservative or fundamentalist approach according to which the final form of the text was given pride of place over against the separate strands of tradition, often in defiance of the new archaeological evidence; and, perhaps most widespread of all, the assumption that chronological priority is the only, or at least the main criterion for determining theological truth or historical authenticity.[22] Whatever the reason, the fact is that this is an important element of biblical tradition which still tends to be overlooked.

2. In addition to this somewhat negative observation that not enough work has been done in modern times on the final form, there is the fact that the finished fabric of the text is as a rule quite intelligible as it stands, and moreover remarkably consistent. This will emerge from the discussion of style below. For the moment one example is enough to illustrate the point.

Psalm 51 'Have mercy on me . . .', is described in the text as 'a psalm of David, when Nathan the prophet came to him after he had gone in to Bathsheba'; and Ps. 127, 'Unless the Lord builds the house . . .', is distinguished from all the other 'Songs of the Temple-steps'[23] by being attributed to Solomon. Since Ps. 51 dates 'probably from the time of Jeremiah' and Ps. 127 'to the more prosperous days of the Greek period', the International Critical Commentary (1907) relegated these and other psalm-headings to the small print, and discussed the psalms without any further reference to the headings.[24] Subsequent commentators adopt a very similar attitude to the problem, quite arbitrarily rejecting this type of situational context as unhistorical, in favour of the settings which modern *Gattungsgeschichte* is able to reconstruct for them.[25] The relation between the situation described in the heading and elements in the psalms, however, while it may be unhistorical and unable to claim any chronological priority, is at least as real and meaningful a relation as that between the modern reconstructed *Sitz im Leben* and the text, and has the advantage over them of being in the text and therefore, perhaps, more amenable to objective analysis. Thus at the level of the final form of the text, the meaning of hara' b^{e}'eneka 'that which is evil in your sight' (Ps. 51.6; EVV 51.4) is defined in terms of David's adultery with Bathsheba and his murder of her husband; and yitten lidido šena 'he gives to his beloved (YADID) sleep' (Ps. 127.2) is beautifully explained by reference to the dream of Solomon (y^{e}didya: II Sam. 12.25) at Gibeon (1 Kings 3.5-15). This is of course only one contextualization of the two psalms, but it is a meaningful one, one that is in the text, and therefore not one to be lightly dismissed.

The specific application of details in the language of the psalms to a bizarre situation in the book of Jonah is another example of the value of a textual setting as well as a reconstructed original one. The conventional imagery of the psalms need not normally have had specific points of reference in any identifiable situation; but in this context it seems that the compiler has intentionally applied a number of these details to Jonah's situation. Indeed one wonders whether the situation, of Jonah inside a big fish, was not invented just to provide points of reference for details in the psalm. Thus 'the belly of Sheol', 'the deep', 'the waters closed over me', 'weeds were wrapped about my head' and other phrases not taken literally in a regular liturgical context, are here given exact points of reference in a fantastic situation, which cannot but draw attention to the more grotesque aspects of some of the stereotyped imagery in the psalms.[26] To take Jonah's prayer out of its textual setting and discuss it only in terms of where it was originally sung, or where it should be contextualized, is again to reject an important and illuminating part of the data.[27]

3. The text in its final form has been the canon of scripture accepted, understood and indeed employed as a rule of life, to a greater or lesser extent, by a number of religious communities for many centuries. The expertise of textual critics and comparative philologists has on occasion blinded us to the plain sense of the text as it stands. Passages which are quite intelligible and which made perfectly good sense to masoretic scholars are described as difficult or impossible or meaningless as they stand. Some of these 'difficulties' are no doubt due to our imperfect knowledge of the ancient Near East, others to a conflict between what we know and what the text says, others to an inadequate knowledge of Hebrew grammar, others to masoretic or earlier Jewish scholarly invention. But, whatever the reason, it is only very rarely that the masoretic text is meaningless. The masoretes saw their task as one of handing down a meaningful text, by whatever strained and artificial methods individual problems demanded, and the result is a definite, for the most part lucid textual tradition, which has been the standard text for most of the religious communities that use the Old Testament.

The word ṣalmawet 'the shadow of death', for example, is perfectly clear as it stands, but raises linguistic and theological problems in its original contexts.[28] ṣal- is irregular as the construct of ṣel 'shadow', and elsewhere is used only in the sense of protection and love, never, as here, in contexts of gloom and danger. Theologically it is hard to prove that Ps. 23.4 was originally about life after death, and there is a good comparative linguistic argument that the word at one time meant 'darkness'. The evidence of the Septuagint, however, makes it clear that 'darkness of death' is ancient. It has also become part of the literature of many languages and to reject it as 'unoriginal' would be not only pedantic, but faulty linguistic method as well, unless the context is first precisely defined. Similarly Amos 3.12, by a charming anachronism, seems to depict the citizens of Samaria as reclining on beds of damask, although this material is first recorded in the tenth century AD. But d^e mešeq is studiously distinguished from dammeśeq 'Damascus' in the masoretic text and makes excellent sense as 'damask', whatever the original text meant.[29]

4. The OT is a religious text, 'the Bible', 'the Word of God', 'Holy Scripture', and as such is to be distinguished from, for example, the Code of Hammurabi or Sennacherib's Annals. Unlike these pieces of ancient Near Eastern literature, which in the same way as some parts of the OT, had specific, identifiable contexts of situation in the ancient Near East, the OT as a whole became a religious text, dissociated from particular situations, and contextualized instead in an infinite number of situations in the history of the synagogue or the church, and in the private experience of individual members of these and other religious communities.

In an interesting study of early Christian iconography,[30] it has been observed that particularity seems to have been purposely kept to a minimum in order to make possible a kind of universal applicability, so that the content could be readily communicated to as many people as possible in as many different situations as possible. This may have been to some extent due to liturgical requirements, but it is certainly true that in most of the Bible there is very little graphic detail: colours are rare, personal appearance is seldom described, detailed topographical descriptions are unusual. This means that an artist may, without doing violence to the text, introduce his own details to make the tradition come home to his contemporaries. He may introduce elements from the liturgy of his time, for example, the altar-table in the scene depicting the sacrifices of Abel and Melchizedek in the Church of San Vitale in Ravenna.[31] Thomas Mann is able to write a monumental epic on *Joseph and His Brethren,* introducing political and psychological factors out of his own and his people's experiences during the period of Nazi domination, without substantially distorting the biblical saga. The language of the Psalms provides another example of this avoidance of particularity: situations are described in such a rich mass of formal, stereotyped expressions, introducing dogs, lions, bulls, oxen, evildoers and the like, sometimes all at the same time (e.g. in Ps. 22), that it is out of the question to attempt to reconstruct one precise, consistent situation in which the psalmist finds himself or imagines himself.

It cannot be finally proved whether this process is always accidental or by design. But the result is that the 'actualization' of biblical traditions or their applicability to a wide variety of different situations is greatly facilitated.[32] One might contrast the universally familiar, formalized language of Matthew 2 or Luke 2 with Christina Georgina Rossetti's hymn 'In the bleak mid-winter', in which circumstantial details tie the same event down to nineteenth-century England, or Leonardo's *Adoration of the Kings,* which is crowded with details of the architecture, culture and religion of fifteenth-century Florence. This wide applicability of biblical tradition is a further argument for choosing the finished article as a starting-point, rather than attempting to reconstruct the original situation or situations with their inevitable particularity.

3. *Linguistic Environment*

The next stage in fixing the context of the terms to be discussed is to decide whether within this corpus there are significant stylistic variations as between one passage and another which might affect the meaning of the terms. From discussion of the wider, situational context, we must now examine the more immediate linguistic environment. It is *a priori* probable, for example, that mošiaʿ in the context of a legal formulation in the Book of Deuteronomy (e.g. 22.27) will have to be defined differently, in terms of associations and overtones, from its usage in the soteriological extravaganzas of one of the classical prophets (e.g. Isa. 49.26). The language of the Hebrew Bible, in other words, is not entirely homogeneous, but contains a number of different varieties. 'Colloquial style', 'Deuteronomic style', 'the language of the law-court', 'early Hebrew poetic style', and the like are familiar enough stylistic labels in OT scholarship; and distinctions of this type are vital, not only for reconstructing the history and religion of ancient Israel, but also in defining the meaning of Hebrew words and phrases.

The task of a word-study is to follow the development and the change of meaning, not in an artificial isolation from the life of Israel, but within the larger framework of the history of the institution.[33]

In biblical research very little has been done on this subject under the name 'stylistics', perhaps because this is a branch of general linguistics which, more even than semantics, is fraught with difficulties and uncertainties.[34] But there have been many attempts to divide up Hebrew into distinct literary units. This is not the place for a detailed critique of these methods as applied to the problem of defining the literary context of a few Hebrew terms. But one feature which most of them have in common must be noted here: they are based on extra-textual criteria, and before accepting them unquestioningly as our starting-point, we must ask whether they are legitimate for the present, unambiguously 'intra-textual' study. For example, a passage described in the text as a prayer addressed to God is classified by the form-critics as a 'hymn' (I Sam. 2.1-10) or a 'thanksgiving psalm' (Jonah 2.3-10; EVV 2.2-9). Similarly, modern historical criteria separate 'early' and 'late' passages which, according to the text, belong together. There is also the distinction between prose and verse. Gesenius-Kautzsch, for example, lists a number of metrical, lexical and syntactical characteristics of the 'poetic language'.[35] But again this distinction is not always beyond dispute. Although not many nowadays would follow Sievers in considering all of Genesis as being written in verse, the RSV does print a considerable number of Genesis passages in verse form.[36] In any case within both prose and verse further styles can be distinguished. BDB, for example, identifies a 'colloquial style', and quotes examples of this both from prose and from poetry, in the earliest strata of Genesis, the exilic literature and the Wisdom tradition.[37] Again this is a stylistic decision taken on extra-textual criteria, and one which we must accept only if it can be shown to have support within the text as well.

The method of stylistic classification suggested here is by reference to 'register' and 'style'.[38] A register is the variety of language proper to a particular situation. Examples of modern written registers would be business letters, newspaper headlines, advertisements, and programme notes. Each of these registers may have within it a number of 'styles', according to a variety of different factors in particular situations: in a study of newspaper headlines for example, it would not be difficult to distinguish the style employed by *The Times* from that of *The Daily Express,* and programme notes by one musicologist or concert pianist would probably be quite unlike those by another. Within a large literary corpus like the OT, one would expect to find distinctions of register and style, and as we shall see, it is remarkable how consistent these distinctions turn out to be.

The register selected here as the linguistic context in which our terms are to be examined is the language variety adopted by people addressing their God. Like the decision on a suitable situational context, this is a purely arbitrary choice, but to be a valid and profitable starting-point it must fulfil certain conditions, and the reasons why this particular register was thought to be a good one for present purposes are as follows.

1. Language addressed to God can be readily identified. It is marked by an introductory formula ('he said to the Lord'), or by the occurrence of one of the names of God in the vocative ('my God', 'O Lord'), or both ('he said to the Lord, "O God . . ." '). In spite of such seemingly fool-proof criteria, however, there is ambiguity in some cases. In many of the psalms and other utterances addressed to God, for instance, there is an abrupt change of person from the second person (addressed to God) to the third person (language about God). This vacillation between persons is a feature which has long been recognized in Biblical Hebrew. Several explanations are customarily offered in the commentaries and grammars. The masoretic text is corrupt (e.g. Gen. 49.4; Lev. 2.8; Isa. 10.12 in BH^3); or 'the alternation between the use of the second person singular and the second person plural immediately indicates breaks in homogeneity. In fact the contents do not make a perfect whole' (von Rad);[39] or in Ps. 93 'the alternation between the hymnic testimony to God (vv.1,4) and the style of prayer (vv.2,5) which depends on the reference of the Psalm to cultic proceedings, produces a vivid

dynamic form, which effectively contrasts with the consistency of the thought-sequence' (Weiser).[40] None of these explanations, however, is legitimate within our present terms of reference: the text as it stands must be understood, wherever possible, without textual emendation; von Rad's reference to the earlier history of the text and Weiser's to its ancient cultic *Sitz im Leben* have nothing to do with the meaning of the final form of the text as contextualized in masoretic tradition. There is one more explanation. This abrupt change of person 'is a primitive stylistic device: a passage begins with purely rhetorical apostrophe, but then the description passes over into the natural third person.'[41] Nyberg accepts this as a feature of OT Hebrew without attempting in the first instance to explain it away or rationalize it. Whether or not it is a 'primitive' device is open to question: it is a regular feature of other languages too, including Ugaritic and Amharic,[42] and if we are right in assuming that some of these changes in person are due to scribal innovations and the juxtaposition of originally separate sources, then we may have to allow that the final form of the text represents a more advanced and sophisticated stage in the development of Hebrew, in which vacillation between persons is not just a mistake, but natural and accepted usage. Whatever the explanation, it is very common in masoretic Hebrew, particularly in the register under discussion, and passages where it occurs are recorded as though they are uniformly addressed to God.

2. This register contains language often consciously distinguished from what precedes and follows it in the text. Some utterances addressed to God are written in a style exactly the same as their literary environment, but many are written in a style which seems to indicate that a special effort is being made on the part of the speaker, aware that he is in the presence of God. This may be indicated in various ways: the speaker's gestures are described (e.g. 'he stood before the altar in the presence of all the assembly of Israel, and spread forth his hands towards heaven, and said . . . ' (I Kings 8.22); there is an abrupt change from prose to verse (e.g. I Sam. 2.1f.; Jonah 2.2f.). This second phenomenon must not be neglected on the grounds that it is due to the activities of an

editor or compiler, or that the reason for the change from prose to verse is simply that the poem has been taken from another context and quite arbitrarily set in its present context in prose narrative. In some contexts the compilers' juxtaposition of what were originally independent units has little or no significance, as in the case of the collections of prophetic utterances grouped on the 'catchword principle'.[43] But in contexts where language is addressed to God, it is clear that the change of style indicates the need for special language when God is being addressed. The compiler has indicated that God is addressed in language proper to the occasion. This is not to say that such language is always in one style: there are prose prayers as well as verse compositions, in a distinct ('Deuteronomic') style[44] (e.g. Dan. 9.4-19; Ezra 9.6-15). The point at issue here is that in Biblical Hebrew a change of style frequently indicates that a speaker is making a special effort to address God in the correct language. In other words we are dealing with a distinct register.

It is interesting to note in passing that the RSV makes a stylistic distinction between this register and the rest of the OT. The archaic 'thou-forms' are consistently used in all language addressed to God. But in so doing, the translators have suggested that there is only one style in the register, while, as we shall see, all utterances addressed to God are not written in the same style, and stylistic distinctions must be established within the register.

3. The register is a particularly interesting one. God is addressed in a very large number of entirely different varieties of language, from querulous colloquialisms (e.g. Gen. 18.15; Ex. 4.13) to highly formalized hymns or prayers (e.g. II Sam. 22.2-51; I Kings 8.23-53; Isa. 38.10-20). The speaker may be anyone from the cultic leader of Israel to a servant-girl, from a lion to the crew of a Phoenician ship (e.g. Ex. 32.11-14; Gen. 16.13; Isa. 21.8; Jonah 1.14), and the location of these utterances varies from the temple in Jerusalem to the belly of a fish (e.g. Ezra 9.6-15 [cf. 10.1]; Jonah 2.2; EVV 2.1).

4. Previous studies of prayer in the OT have tended to confine themselves either to the examination of various

relevant literary forms (e.g. *Klagelieder*, 'prose-prayers'), which cover only a small number of the utterances addressed to God,[45] or to etymological studies which begin not from the actual utterances themselves, but from the various words for 'prayer' and 'to pray' in Biblical Hebrew.[46] To the present writer's knowledge there has been no complete survey of all the language addressed to God.

5. Finally, for obvious reasons, the form-critics have not devoted equal amounts of energy to all utterances addressed to God. Poetic passages have been the subject of much more form-critical analysis than prose. More work has been done on the detailed analysis of the *Sitz im Leben* of the psalms than on the situational context of other parts of the OT. The present method reverses the balance, since prose passages often provide fuller and more precise introductory formulae, which describe the situational context of the utterances much more fully and objectively than some of the hypothetical reconstructions of the form-critics.

The first stage in the classification was to assemble all the utterances in the register. Many of these could then be grouped, according to their introductory formulae (e.g. wayyitpallel yona ʾel YHWH wayyoʾmer . . .), into 'HITPALLEL-utterances'), 'QARA-utterances', etc. Of the fourteen groups thus distinguished five were set aside on the grounds that none of the terms to be discussed occurs in them, and we find only one, or at most two, examples of each in the OT.[47] The remaining nine were examined for distinctive contextual and linguistic features, and it soon became apparent that there was a remarkable consistency within each group which suggested a possible method of defining styles within the register without recourse to extra-textual criteria. This is a contextual classification and as such would fit the following definition of style or one similar to it: 'The style of a text is the aggregate of the contextual probabilities of its linguistic items',[48] probabilities because the evidence in the corpus is limited, and contextual in accordance with our decision to begin from the final form of the text.

1. HITPALLEL-style (Deut. 9.26-9; I Sam. 2.1-10; II Kings 6.17-20; II Kings 19.15-19 = Isa. 37.16-20; II Kings 20.3 = Isa. 38.3; Jer. 32.17-25; Jonah 2.2-9; 4.2f.; Neh. 1.5-11; cf.

also the following T^e PILLOT 'prayers'; II Sam. 7.18-29 = I Chron. 17.16-29; I Kings 8.23-53 = II Chron. 6.14-42; Hab. 3.2-15; Dan. 9.4-19; Ezra 9.6-15). With very few exceptions (II Kings 6; Jer. 32; Jonah 2,4) HITPALLEL-utterances are associated with cultic locations or activities. The speakers are normally the leaders of Israel, kings and prophets. The patriarchs' prayers (Gen. 28.20-22; 32.9-13) are not described as HITPALLEL-utterances, nor are those of the minor characters in the OT, like Abraham's servant (Gen. 24.12-14), the idolatrous craftsmen ridiculed by Isaiah (44.17) and the sailors in Jonah 1.14. Utterances in this group are of a considerable length or substance (except II Kings 6); the vocative occurs in every case (except I Sam. 2); abrupt changes of person are quite frequent, and the terms HOŠIA', HIṢṢIL, etc. occur frequently too. Common to many of them are confession of sin, declaration of faith in God and intercession for the community. They are all, in short, written in a distinctive style, we shall call it a 'set-piece' style, usually distinguished quite clearly from its compositional framework. This consistent stylistic picture is supported by modern criteria as well, whereby nearly all of the HITPALLEL-utterances are defined as either psalms (I Sam. 2; Jonah 2; Hab. 3) or 'Deuteronomic prayers' (Deut. 9; II Sam. 7; I Kings 8; II Kings 19; Jer. 32; Dan. 9; Ezra 9; Neh. 1). Of the few exceptions, one has some Deuteronomic features (II Kings 20), and another is certainly intended to be taken as a set-piece (Jonah 4.2f.), contextualized in a grotesque situation in the same way as the psalm in Jonah 2.[49]

2. ŠA'AL (DARAŠ)-style (Judg. 1.1; 20.18; I Sam. 10.22; 14.37; 23.2; 30.8; II Sam. 2.1; 5.19 = I Chron. 14.10; I Kings 22.6,15 = II Chron. 18.5,14; II Kings 1.2; 8.8). All these utterances are set in the period between the death of Joshua and the time of Elisha. In all except the pre-monarchical passages, the king is the speaker; a cultic context is normally specified. They are all short and consist of interrogative sentences, often in pairs (I Sam. 14; II Sam. 2; 5.19; I Kings 22); and the name of God is never mentioned. We may assume that some traces of the proper style for 'oracular questions' have survived here. The absence of a vocative may reflect a procedure whereby God was addressed through an

intermediary.[50]

3. QARA'-style (Judg. 15.18; 16.28; I Kings 17.20,21; Isa. 21.8; Jonah 1.14; I Chron. 4.10; II Chron. 14.10. Cf. also Gen. 16.13; Jer. 3.4,19; Hos. 2.18). There is no indication that QARA'-utterances had any association with cultic locations or activities. They are all short (except Isa. 21). The vocative occurs at the beginning of all the utterances in this group except three, which are exceptional in other ways as well. These are Judg. 15.18, where QARA' is used to provide an etymological explanation of the spring at '<u>en</u> <u>haqqore</u>'; and need have no stylistic significance, and two passages which have long puzzled commentators, Isa. 21.8 in which the speaker is a lion (<u>'arie</u>), and I Chron. 4.10, the only piece of oratio recta in the Chronicler's genealogies (1-8) and the only reference in the OT to Jabez as a person. The prominence of the vocative in all the other short QARA'-utterances suggests a connexion with four 'naming utterances' (Gen. 16.13; Jer. 3.4,19; Hos. 2.18) which are introduced by the same or a similar formula; and it may be suggested that this style was an extension of simple invocations of God by name.[51] This was a feature of prayer apparently considered distinctive enough to warrant a special aetiology among the legends of Genesis (4.26b).

4. ṢA'AQ-style (Ex. 17.14; Num. 12.13; Judg. 10.10; 10.15; I Sam. 12.10; Ezek. 11.13; Hos. 8.2). This style is similar to the QARA'-style, in that the utterances are all short and have no specific association with the cult. The vocative, however, is much less common (only Ezek. 11; Hos. 8; Num. 12). Five of the seven passages may incorporate ancient ritual formulations (Num. 12; Judg. 10.10,15; I Sam. 12; Hos. 8.2), and the ṢA'AQ-style would then be distinguishable from the more conventional HITPALLEL-style on one hand, and the invocations described above as QARA'-utterances.

5. NADAR-style (Gen. 28.20-22; Num. 21.2; Judg. 11.30f.; I Sam. 1.11). All four NADAR-utterances occur in premonarchical contexts. They are all short, and the vocative appears in only one of them (I Sam. 1). They all consist of a protasis introduced by <u>'im</u>, and an apodosis with pleonastic <u>waw</u>.

6. ŠIR-style (Ex. 15.1b-18; Judg. 5.2-31a; II Sam. 22.2-51 = Ps. 18.3-51; Isa. 26.1b-21). Three of the utterances in this group occur in contexts described by the emotive phrase bay-yom hahu' 'on that day', referring to the miracle at the Red Sea (Ex. 15), Deborah's victory at Taanach (Judg. 5) and the resurrection of the dead (Isa. 26). The fourth passage occurs in the context of a kind of appendix in which various poems, lists of warriors and the like have been collected (II Sam. 22-23). All four passages are of considerable length; there are no imperatival sentences; the vocative occurs frequently; there are abrupt changes of person; the terms HOŠIA', HIṢṢIL, etc. occur frequently in Ex. 15 and II Sam. 22.

7. BEREK-style (Gen. 49.2-27; Deut. 33.2-29). Both 'blessings' occur at the end of the book in which they are included; and in both cases the speaker is at the very end of his life. Both are long and complex compositions; the vocative occurs only three times; imperatival sentences are frequent; there are many abrupt changes of person; there is a declaration of faith in God (Gen. 49.18; Deut. 33.26).

8. 'ANA-style (Deut. 21.7f.; 26.5-10). Both utterances occur among legal formulations in Deuteronomy; both are accompanied by ritual, and both contain formulae prescribed for particular situations (an unsolved murder-case and an Israelite's arrival in the promised land).

9. MIKTAB (Isa. 38.9-20). The context of Hezekiah's words was apparently some kind of thanksgiving ritual (vv.19f.) after he had recovered from an illness. The abrupt change from the narrative style to a 'set-piece' style, characterized by the length and complexity of the composition, the frequent abrupt changes of person and the occurrence of HOŠIA' (v.20), marks this utterance as stylistically close to the HITPALLEL-utterances (cf. Jonah 2).

Of the nine 'styles' that we have attempted to distinguish in the register, using precise introductory formulae as our criteria, the single utterance (9) is indistinguishable from other passages in the HITPALLEL-style, with which it may now be grouped, and three more, (2), (5) and (8), need not concern us since none of the terms under discussion occur in them. This leaves five styles, all of which have two remarkable features in common: they exhibit enough contextual and linguistic features to permit generalizations on the style in which they are written, and, equally significant, they are almost invariably distinguishable from the style of the language immediately preceding and following them. In other words we may legitimately speak of five set-piece styles in our register.

Of the other 150 or so passages addressed to God in the OT, 82 are best described as conversational in style.[52] In these there is no evidence that any special effort is made on the part of the speaker in God's presence: God is addressed exactly as though he were a member of the same language-community as the speaker. The introductory formula is of the type wayyo'mer . . . 'and he said'; there is no evidence of cultic gestures accompanying the utterance or that it is a cultic official speaking or that the situation was a cultic location. About half of these passages occur in the Pentateuch. They are particularly frequent in Jeremiah, Zechariah, and Malachi, and totally absent from the eighth-century prophets. Most of the utterances are short; the vocative is rare; HOŠIAʿ occurs only once (Judg. 6), HIṢṢIL once (Gen. 32.31); and MILLEṬ once (Gen. 19.19).

We find 26 utterances, also introduced by the neutral wayyo'mer 'and he said', set in contexts clearly described as cultic.[53] Those that contain any of the terms to be defined are readily grouped with our stylistic prototypes as follows:

1. HITPALLEL-style: I Chron. 16.35; II Chron. 20.6-12.
2. ṢAʿAQ-style: Jer. 2.27.

Of the other utterances in the register which have no special introductory formula or cultic associations, but exhibit enough characteristics to suggest a 'set-piece' style,[54] only two are relevant as containing the terms HIṢṢIL and YᵉŠUʿA, and may be classified as follows:

1. HITPALLEL: Gen. 32. 9-13.
2. ŠIR: Isa. 12.

Finally, there is a group of 37 passages in the register which have no introductory formula at all.[55] These are incorporated into longer utterances from which they are often stylistically indistinguishable. They are in effect examples of that abrupt change of person which we have seen to be a characteristic of much of the register in Biblical Hebrew. But whereas other utterances containing this change of person are apparently addressed *in toto* to God, here only those parts composed in the second person masculine singular are addressed to God, the rest of the passage being expressly addressed to someone else (e.g. an enemy in Isa. 33.1f.; the reader in Neh. 5.19), or spoken by someone else (e.g. Jer. 17.18f.). Most of these passages fall naturally into the stylistic patterns outlined above, and the six that concern us as containing the terms HOŠIA‘ and Y^E ŠU‘A are all typical HITPALLEL-utterances: Isa. 33.2-4; 63.7-64.11; Jer. 3.22-25; 14.7-9; 17.13-18; Hab. 1.2-4.[56]

In the interests of objectivity and precision we have begun this study in semantics by narrowing our terms of reference as far as possible. First, the contextualization of Biblical Hebrew in masoretic tradition was distinguished from other situational contexts in which the terms under discussion have meaning; and now, second, we have defined a register and, within it, a set of styles, which have enough formal characteristics to be described as ‘set-piece’ styles. The incidence of the terms HOŠIA‘, HIṢṢIL, etc. in this set-piece variety of Biblical Hebrew is given in Table 1. Their incidence in conversational style addressed to God is also included in this table.

TABLE ONE

Incidence of HOŠIAʿ, HIṢṢIL, *etc. in the register*

Style	HITPALLEL	QARAʾ	ṢAʿAQ	ŠIR	BEREK	Conver-sational
HOŠIAʿ	I Sam. 2.1. II Kings 19.19 Isa. 33.2 37.20 38.20 64.4 Jer. 3.23 14.8 14.9 17.14 Jonah 2.10 Hab. 1.2 3.8 3.13 3.18 I Chron. 16.35 16.35 II Chron. 6.41 20.9	Judg. 15.18	Jer. 2.27c Hos. 14.4	Ex. 15.2 II Sam. 22.3 22.3 22.3 22.4 22.28 22.36 22.42 22.47 22.51 Isa. 12.2 12.2 12.3 26.1	Gen. 49.18 Deut. 33.29	Judg. 6.36
HIṢṢIL	Gen. 32.12 Isa. 44.17		Judg. 10.15 I Sam. 12.10	II Sam. 22.18 22.49		Gen. 32.31
ʿAZAR		II Chron. 14.10 14.10		Judg. 5.23	Gen. 49.25 Deut. 33.7 33.26 33.29	
PILLEṬ	Lam. 2.22 Ezra 9.8 9.13 9.14 9.15			II Sam. 22.2 22.44		
MILLEṬ						Gen. 19.20
ḤILLEṢ				II Sam. 22.20		
PARAQ	Lam. 5.8					
PAṢA						

Nominalizations are underlined

III

SEMANTIC FIELDS

Structural semantics still lags behind the rest of general linguistics, but this is not to say, as some do, that there has been no adequate formulation of a general semantic theory applicable to any linguistic data.[1] There have been two main approaches to the problem: broadly speaking, the first consists of vocabulary analysis, the second of context-analysis. Representative of the first is S. Ullmann,[2] but it would be true to say that the main interest in most traditional semantic theory (e.g. Kronasser, Guiraud, Struck)[3] is the lexicon rather than the text.[4] Lyons' analysis of part of the vocabulary of Plato is representative of the second approach, and Chapter IV takes his *Structural Semantics* as its starting-point.[5] The aims of the 'lexis-experiment' in Edinburgh, interest in collocability (Firth, Halliday) and important definitions of situation (Urban, Ellis, Ziff) are also context-based.[6]

This distinction is by no means a clear-cut one, and it would be misleading to suggest that semanticists fall precisely into one or other of two 'schools'. But from the practical point of view the distinction is important: whether one should begin from the lexicon and work from there to the text, or from the text and work towards precise lexicographical definition. On the one hand, one can begin by attempting to discover in the vocabulary of a language 'semantic universals', i.e. features and processes common to all languages, like the distinction between transparent and opaque words, metaphorical transfer, taboo, and linguistic borrowing.[7] Although some of these phenomena can be described as synchronic, they are best examined as historical factors which affect the meaning of words. A historical change in meaning, for example, evident in ŠAPAṬ 'to judge' may be due to a recurring relation of synonymy with HOŠIA', and, if so, this is the important point, not just the synchronic fact of synonymy.[8]

On the other hand, the context-based approach is, in contrast with the first, exclusively synchronic. Meaning-relations like synonymy, opposition, implication and reference, are entirely dependent on the context: words that are synonyms in one context may not be synonyms in another.[9] By context, here, is meant not only a word's situational context and its literary context as outlined in the previous chapter, but also its immediate linguistic environment; and semantic description of a word consists primarily of a careful analysis of the contexts in which it occurs. The meaning of HOŠIA', for example, can be defined in terms of its almost exclusive collocation with God, its frequent synonymous relation with HIṢṢIL, and its equally frequent opposition to ṢAR, MAWET etc. The analysis of contexts along these lines distinguishes the word from HIṢṢIL, and produces a definition of the meaning as it is applied in the contexts available.

Now this is the approach advocated by John Lyons in his *Structural Semantics.* But by confining one's attention too rigidly to the immediate lexical environment, there is a danger that historical factors which affect the meaning of a word are ignored: these are factors which operate (or have already operated) outside the word's immediate linguistic environment. It may be that the relative importance of a word's history in its contextual meaning varies from word to word, and from style to style. But allowance must be made for historical factors. The plea for 'panchronic semantics' does not imply a blurring of the distinction between historical (diachronic) and synchronic semantics. It is intended to indicate the need for semantic description from both points of view.[10] It is for this reason that the detailed context-based analysis of the meaning of HOŠIA', HIṢṢIL, etc.[11] is preceded by an examination of that section of the Biblical Hebrew vocabulary to which they belong.

1. *The Associative Field of HOŠIA'*

One of the most illuminating discoveries of twentieth-century linguistics is that a word can be fruitfully examined against the background of its 'semantic field'. 'Field theory', first formulated by Trier in 1931, introduced an important new concept into the study and description of meaning.[12] It was immediately seized upon by neo-Humboldtian philosophers, who attempted to derive ethnolinguistic conclusions from it; theories of the relation between language and the *Weltbild* were constructed upon it, and the original theory, along with its practical implications for organizing vocabulary and analysing semantic developments, brought into disrepute. Forty years of development and modification have removed some of the excessively literal interpretations of the theory, and produced a balanced approach to several of the crucial problems of semantics.[13] Since its application to OT Hebrew is still in its infancy,[14] and the field to which HOŠIA' belongs provides an exceptionally rich and interesting example, an examination of the field is preceded by some account of the method and its contribution to biblical semantics.

> Dans l'intérieur d'une même langue tous les mots qui expriment des idées voisines se limitent réciproquement: des synonymes . . . n'ont leur valeur propre que par leur opposition.[15]

Since de Saussure, 'opposition' has been an essential principle in semantic theory. The mapping out of a word's associative field is in effect a graphic way of putting this principle into operation. Synonymy and opposition are not the only meaning-relations to be considered in defining a word's meaning; but the vagueness of de Saussure's expression 'des idées voisines' makes allowance for this and is in perfect accord with the fluidity of a field's boundaries. An 'associative field' would include all the words associated in any way with a particular term. It has been described as 'a halo which surrounds the sign and whose outer fringes merge into their environment',[16] and must be distinguished from a 'lexical field' or 'group', which can be precisely defined for any given corpus. While a word's associative field includes terms related to it at all levels (for instance synonyms, opposites, terms that rhyme with it or look like it), a lexical group consists only of words very closely related to one another. Thus we shall speak of the

'HOŠIA'-field', which incorporates 200 or more items, while 'HOŠIA', HIṢṢIL, etc.' is a much smaller lexical group (within the associative field). Trier's work was on the smaller groupings, which he and his followers claim correspond to conceptual spheres. In each lexical field some sphere of reality or experience is organized in a unique way, and from a comparative study of such fields as between one language and another, or between one period and another within the same language, conclusions on the way the speakers of that language think are derived. We shall return to this question later. Meanwhile, the fluidity and great size of an associative field, as opposed to lexical fields, must not blind us to the essential advantages of the notion.

This is a method of organizing vocabulary which takes into account the nature of language more adequately than any other.[17] The alternative is the alphabetical lexicon, in which words are listed according to an entirely arbitrary principle. In Semitic lexicography this has produced some odd and, on occasion, misleading results. In BDB, for example, words are listed according to their roots: thus not only is the alphabetical arrangement alien to the words, but many of the forms listed (root *in vacuo*) are not attested in Biblical Hebrew. The result is that pride of place is irreversibly given to the etymology of a word, even where the etymology is obscure. In BDB, for instance, 'ARBE 'locust' comes under I. RABA 'to be much, many, great'; ḤIṬṬA 'wheat' under ḤANAṬ 'to spice'; 'ET 'time' under I. 'ANA 'to answer, respond'. In not every case does the lay-out of such a dictionary affect the meaning of a word, but one example of where it does is the word HOŠIA'. In this case the etymology, although it is one which is not accepted without reservation by the lexicographers,[18] has become an integral part of the meaning of the word in modern biblical scholarship. If the word was seen against the background of its associative field, instead of a hypothetical reconstruction of its prehistory, its meaning might be greatly clarified.

Another source of confusion and semantic distortion is the prominence given to translation in traditional lexical work. Here again field theory helps to avoid a common error, by dealing with the meaning of words from within the language.

Naturally no two languages would be expected to have fields of exactly the same size: this is one reason why loan-words occur, to fill gaps in particular fields. This is why, for instance, Hebraisms occur in English: the HOŠIA'-field in Hebrew is far larger than its equivalent in English and has accordingly produced, in the Authorized Version, expressions like 'thou hast enlarged me when I was in distress' (Ps. 4.2) and 'the lifter up of mine head' (Ps. 33). The semantic spread of English 'answer' is limited by the co-presence of the word 'testify', unlike 'ANA 'to answer, to testify', which belongs to the HOŠIA'-field. This makes translation difficult (although not impossible), but elucidates the meaning of the word in Hebrew. Instead of defining a word L in terms of another language, it can be defined as associated with A, B, C (in the same language), opposed to D, influenced semantically by G because of frequent collocation with it in idiom I, and so on. This is the most reliable method of describing meaning, and must precede translation, not follow it.

Finally, there is the uneasy problem of concept-studies. A detailed study of the root *ZKR, for example, professes also to be a study of *'Gedenken' im alten Orient und im Alten Testament; Die Hauptbegriffe für Sünde* are in effect the main OT words for sin;[19] among the articles in Kittel's *Theological Dictionary of the New Testament,* it is often not clear whether the author is defining the meaning of the word at the head of the article, or discussing the concept which it sometimes denotes.[20] The assumption that there is an exact one-to-one correspondence between a word and its conceptual referent (e.g. 'der Begriff paša'/peša')[21] is by no means universally accepted. Until it is, a study of memory in the OT must include, not just ZAKAR 'to remember' (still less the root *in vacuo* *ZKR), but also ŠAKAḤ 'to forget', and DIMMA 'to actualize' (?), at least. Ps. 48.10 (EVV 48.9) for example, which is clearly important for a study of memory in the OT, is not referred to in any of the three recent studies of the subject.[22] A minute description of the ZAKAR-field is what is required and the systematic classification of all the memory-contexts (instead of just those in which ZAKAR happens to occur). What is the meaning of ZAKAR in OT Hebrew? and What is OT teaching about memory? are different questions. To answer both of them the theory of semantic fields is a help, but for the second it is essential. The present study is primarily concerned with a question of the first type, What is the meaning of HOŠIA', HIṢṢIL, etc.? but in describing the associative field to which these words belong, some steps will be taken in the direction of producing an answer to the question, What is OT teaching about salvation?

In OT Hebrew studies several fields have already been the subject of detailed examination: e.g. words for time, geographical terminology, ceramic vocabulary.[23] Scharfstein's *Thesaurus* groups Hebrew vocabulary in fields arranged alphabetically under one word from each, and the present study is a description of another lexical field, namely HOŠIA', HIṢṢIL, etc.

The problem of deciding which words belong to such a study and which do not, is not an easy one. Semantic developments can occur within a relatively confined lexical grouping, but also within a far wider field. Should not 'Biblical Words for Time', for instance, be extended to include such words as 'ARAK 'to endure', matay 'when', l^e^panim 'before', miqqedem 'of old', and so on? Is not some account of words like ŠAPAṬ, ROMEM, which are associated with HOŠIA', HIṢṢIL, etc., essential to a complete description of the meaning of HOŠIA'?

It is here that the wider concept of the 'associative field', as distinct from the narrower lexical group, is valuable. In the first place many linguistic phenomena occur not just in relation to synonyms or the like, but also with opposites. Various types of interference are liable to occur among words associated by any one of the meaning-relations, not just the obvious ones. This means that the definition of the boundaries of an associative field will be fluid. To give an approximate idea of the size of such a field, a French linguist showed that the associative field of the word *chat* 'cat' comprises about 2000 words.[24]

The criteria for building up this far larger field are in the last resort intuitive. Attempts to formulate a complete, watertight pattern of semantic fields, including the whole lexicon of a language, have been made, and naturally when dealing with a closed corpus like the OT, this is theoretically straightforward.[25] But it would not be possible, or indeed desirable, to define in exact terms the processes whereby all associated lexical items, words and longer phrases, are recognized.

The intuitive element in linguistic work has been questioned as to whether it can legitimately be used in the scientific investigation. The first answer to this charge is that intuition, imagination and hypothesis, far from being written off as 'unscientific', are now being acknowledged more and more as essential factors in scientific progress. At a recent international congress of astrophysicists, for example, the reading of science fiction was seriously recommended as an aid to solving scientific problems. But more important, in linguistic research intuition can be said to play a less subjective role than it does in other disciplines, because a large proportion of the decisions made independently by millions of people every day are intuitive, and yet yield the same result in almost every case. Intuition in other words plays a vital role in mutual intelligibility. People make and understand utterances they have never heard before and in the same way the present writer's knowledge of Hebrew is an important factor in the situation (however hard to prove or define), so that a classification of Hebrew vocabulary based on it is a possible starting-point, and, what is more, one on which there would be a very large measure of agreement, one might venture to suggest, among similarly informed writers and scholars.[26]

A knowledge of Hebrew implies that I can intuitively recognize words of related meaning. It is unimportant whether such empirical observations are due to the fact that I know I can translate them into another language by the same word; or whether it is because I have noticed they occur in similar contexts regularly, or refer to identical extra-lingual features; possibly it is because I have discovered that they occur within the structure of Hebrew poetry in such a way as to show a semantic relationship between them. All these factors will be examined in due course; but the first step is to build up the associative field without precise, mechanical methods. In accordance with the well-tried dictum *σῴζειν τὰ φαινόμενα*, the analysis of the associative field of HOŠIA', thus compiled, can be considered an adequate and at the same time an interesting and promising starting-point, although Ziff's corollary to *σῴζειν τὰ φαινόμενα*, namely, *miracula sine doctrina nihil valent*,[27] nicely emphasizes the fact that intuition is only a starting-point for semantic analysis, and no more.

Since we shall be primarily concerned only with the central core of the field to which HOSIAʿ and its immediate lexical neighbours belong, what is required now is a general description of its wider associative field. Some conclusions will be drawn concerning the relative importance of each part of the field in OT language about salvation, the context in which it is applied (e.g. mortal danger, illness, war, guilt, ignorance), and the concepts or theological categories which it is used to describe. In effect this will be a general study of OT language about salvation. Unlike traditional concordance-based studies which take one or two 'key-words', it will be concerned with as many as possible of the 'salvation contexts', irrespective of the words occurring in them. It does not profess to present a complete picture, but may nonetheless serve to illustrate the advantages of a more comprehensive approach to the language of the OT.

The central core of the field consists of the following:

HOŠIAʿ, yešaʿ, y^{e}šuʿa, mošiaʿ, mošaʿot, t^{e}šuʿa;
HIṢṢIL, haṣṣala;
ʿAZAR, ʿezer, ʿezra;
ḤILLEṢ;
MILLEṬ;
PILLEṬ, palleṭ, paliṭ, paleṭ, p^{e}leṭa;
PAṢA;
PARAQ.

These words make up the lexical group which is the subject of detailed analysis in Chapter IV. It comprises the minimum lexical group on which a discussion of OT Language about salvation can be based.

It may appear strange that ʿAZAR 'to help' is included in this minimal core of the field. In fact, as we shall see, HOŠIAʿ is in some respects semantically closer to ʿAZAR than it is to, for instance, HIṢṢIL.

Associated with this central core is a large, heterogeneous stock of lexical items, designated 'the HOŠIAʿ-field'. Most of these can be readily grouped as terms derived from a forensic context or the military sphere or the like. A dozen such groups can be identified within the field, but this still leaves a considerable number of words like 'AHEB 'to love', YADA' 'to know', ZAKAR 'to remember', BAḤAR 'to choose', which have an obvious association with HOŠIA', HIṢṢIL, etc., and which all have this in common, that they generally denote an attitude, rather than an activity, on the part of the subject towards the object. These items are grouped in one comprehensive sector which may conveniently be headed by the neutral word YADA' 'to know' (see Table 2).

An element in this field which would have relevance for a discussion of the etymology of HOŠIA' is 'spaciousness'. A detailed study of this sector indicates its importance and rich applicability in OT language about salvation.[28] What bearing does this have on the popular etymology which explains HOŠIA' by reference to Arabic wasi'a 'to be spacious'. It would have been very satisfying, for instance, to discover that HOŠIA' was semantically closer to this sector than to any of the others. This is, however, by no means the case: indeed it occurs noticeably less often in collocation with ṣar than HIṢṢIL does, and in the frequent soteriological passages where words for 'spacious' or 'to give room to' occur, HOŠIA' is conspicuous by its absence.[29]

We shall have occasion, secondly, to discuss the frequency of metaphorical transference from the forensic sphere into the HOŠIA'-field. While GA'AL and PADA correspond closely both grammatically and semantically to HOŠIA', we shall see how ŠAPAṬ, RIB, 'ANA, and DIN have been influenced by their proximity to HOŠIA'.[30] We might add nominal forms like GO'EL, ŠOPEṬ and ṢADDIQ attested in soteriological contexts, where, as in English 'redeemer', the original forensic sense of the words has virtually disappeared. HOŠIA' itself may be another example of this development, and a picture of the HOŠIA'-field as it was at an earlier stage in the development of the language might have shown the 'lawcourt' sector in the centre, the more general usage of HOŠIA' not yet having been established.[31]

PAṢA 'to save' may be an 'Aramaism',[32] but it is important to notice that a similar development is also attested in OT Hebrew, where PITTEAḤ 'to open' occurs in the HOŠIA'-field.[33] The problem of distinguishing between true semantic borrowing and parallel developments in neighbouring lan-

Table 2 Part of the Associative Field of HOŠIAʿ in Old Testament Hebrew

Spaciousness

HIRḤIB	Ps. 4.2(1)
HIPTA	Gen. 9.27
RAWAḤ	Job. 32.20

Healing

RAPA’	Jer. 17.14
ḤIYYA	Ps. 119.25
ḤABAŠ	Isa. 61.1
HE‘ᵉLA ’ªRUKA	Jer. 30.17

Support

SAMAK	Ps. 3.6(5)
TAMAK	Ps. 41.13(12)
SA‘AD	Ps. 18.36(35)
NE’ᵉMAN	II Chron. 20.20

Leading

HINḤA	Deut. 32.12
NEHEL	Isa. 49.10
ŠUB Šᵉ BUT	Deut. 30.3
NAḤA	Ex. 15.13
HEKIN PA‘AM	Ps. 119.133

Lawcourt

GA’AL	Ps. 119.114
PADA	Ps. 78.42
DIN	Ps. 54.3(1)
‘ANA	Ps. 22.22(21)
ŠAPAṬ	Isa. 33.22
RIB	I Sam. 24.16
QAROB ṢEDEQ	Isa. 51.5
GOZE(?)	Ps. 71.6
ṢIWWA(?)	Ps. 71.3

HOŠIAʿ	MILLEṬ
HIṢṢIL	ḤILLEṢ
‘AZAR	PAṢA
PILLEṬ	PARAQ

Knowing

YADA‘	Amos 3.2
’AHEB	Hos. 3.1
BAḤAR	Isa. 44.1
ZAKAR	Ps. 106.4
HIBBIṬ	Ps. 102.20(19)
ḤAŠAQ	Deut. 7.7
ḤANAN	Ps. 4.2(1)
‘AŚA ḤESED	Ps. 18.51(50)
BEREK	Ps. 128.5

Keeping

NAṢAR	Ps. 32.7
ḤAŚAK	Ps. 19.14(13)
ŠAMAR	Ps. 121.5

Cleaning

ṬEHER	Ps. 51.4(2)
ḤIṬṬE’	Ps. 51.9(7)
KIBBEŚ	Ps. 51.9(7)
MAḤA	II Kings 21.13

Light

BA’’OR	Isa. 61.1
‘ARAK NER	Ps. 132.17
HIGGIAH ḤOŠEK	Ps. 18.29(28)
HE’IR	Ps. 118.27

Lifting

MAŠA	Ps. 18.17 (16)
DILLA	Ps. 30.2 (1)

Military

GANAN	II Kings 19.34
NILḤAM	Ex. 14.14
LABAŠ ŠIRYON	Isa. 59.17
ḤANA SABIB	Ps. 34.8(7)

Refining

ŚARAP	Isa. 1.25
ZIQQEQ	Mal. 3.3

Opening

PITTEAḤ	Ps. 102.21(20)
ŠIBBER DELET	Ps. 107.16

ROMEM	Ps. 27.5
HE‘ᵉLA	Ps. 40.3(2)
ŚIGGEB	Ps. 107.41
HE‘ᵉMID ‘al BAMOT	Ps. 18.34(33)

Verse numbers in brackets are those of EVV

guages is well-known.[34]

Several puzzles can best be explained against their background in an associative field like that of HOŠIA‘. We are primarily concerned with HOŠIA‘, and this is therefore not the place for detailed discussions of peripheral words. A few examples, however, will be briefly examined in order to illustrate further the value of this type of lexical grouping.

Two terms in Ps. 71 have long perplexed commentators. First, ṣiwwita in Ps. 71.3 is said to be meaningless and a corruption of l^e bet m^e ṣudot.[35] Seen alongside Ps. 44.5 (EVV 44.4), however, and against the background of the HOŠIA‘-field, ṣiwwita l^e hoši‘eni is surely another example of the metaphorical application of a forensic term to an act of divine intervention. The translation might be:

Your command is my salvation.[36]

The second term is gozi in Ps. 71.6:

5. For thou, O Lord, art my hope,
   my trust, O Lord, from my youth.
6. Upon thee I have learned from my birth;
   thou gozi from my mother's womb.

Proposed solutions involve either emending the text or taking 'from my mother's womb' in a quite different sense from the two parallel expressions 'from my youth' and 'from my birth'.[37] It is clear that in these two verses, the four terms for 'to hope', 'to trust', 'to support' and gozi belong together, so that gozi, like the other three, belongs to the HOŠIA‘-field. Now in the 'lawcourt' sector of the field there are three words for 'to cut' used, like Latin *decido* and German *entscheiden,* in the sense 'to decide, to decree'.[38] These are ḤAQAQ, ḤATAK and GAZAR. It seems possible that in goze we have another, corresponding to m^e ḥoqeq 'commander', in which the semantic development ḤAQAQ 'to cut' ḤAQAQ 'to command' is well established. The verb of GAZA 'to cut' does not occur in OT Hebrew, although it is attested in Aramaic, but the noun gazit is common enough in collocation with ’abne 'hewn stones'. The existence of a biform of GAZAZ is feasible whether it happens to occur in OT Hebrew or not, and the participle goze would then be 'the one who cuts, i.e. decrees'.

We might suggest the following translation for the verse:

Thou hast been my protector since before I was born.

'Protector' is an appropriate English equivalent since its technical application, like that of gozi, belongs to the term's prehistory (that is to say, seventeenth-century English), while an extended, soteriological sense is what is required by the context.[39] No claim is being made here that this is necessarily the correct solution to the problem; its importance for the present discussion is that it came to light as a direct result of an examination of the relevant semantic field.

Another example concerns the relation between HENIAḤ 'to give rest to' and NAḤA/HINḤA 'to lead'. HENIAḤ is not easily translated 'to give rest to' in several contexts, where movement is indicated: e.g. Isa. 63.14, where it occurs in parallel to NIHAG 'to lead', and is emended by some commentators.[40] BDB suggests 'to give rest to, i.e. bring to a resting-place'. Again it seems that too great a reliance on translation has caused this confusion, while a monolingual approach to the problem provides a possible solution. It will be noticed that in the 'leading' sector of the HOŠIA'-field the word NEHAL occurs. This word also requires two unexpectedly diverse translations: (1) 'to lead' and (2) 'to give rest to, refresh'.[41] In other words the semantic range of HENIAḤ as described above is no wider than that of NEHAL. This leads to the further conclusion that NUAḤ and NAḤA are biforms like ḤUM/ḤAMA, 'UR/'ARA, ŠUAḤ/ŠAḤA, etc., and the rather unsatisfactory attempts that have been made to distinguish them etymologically and semantically are rendered unnecessary.[42]

One final example, of a different kind, is the expression babboqer 'in the morning'. Two main interpretations have been offered according to which the phrase either refers to a specific time in a liturgical sequence or in a historical event, or was not intended to denote anything more precise than 'right early'.[43] A third possibility emerges from a glance at the 'light' sector. Like 'OR, ŠEMEŠ and the others, metaphorical transference brings BOQER into the HOŠIA'-field. Thus 'in the morning', that is, like the sun, God intervenes in situations of darkness and danger, and the wicked are dispersed like creatures of the night:

Have you commanded the morning since your days began,
and caused the dawn to know its place,
that it might take hold of the skirts of the earth,
and the wicked be shaken out of it? (Job 38.12f.)

It is remarkable, in view of this famous passage, that the possibility of a metaphorical use of BOQER has not been adduced, especially when it does not necessarily preclude a liturgical origin for this type of language. To this and other problems concerning the origin of certain lexical features of OT Hebrew we shall now turn.

The relation between language and culture is a well worn problem and one which this is not the place to tackle.[44] It is obviously dangerous to base any conclusion concerning the cultural or religious conditions of a people on the presence or absence of one word in their language as in the following example: 'Greek thought, for instance, had no idea of the righteousness of God as a divine activity bringing about salvation'.[45] It would be absurd, for example, to draw any conclusions about personal hygiene in ancient Israel from the fact that there is no general word for 'dirty' in OT Hebrew. There are two words for 'dirty' applied only to water (DALAḤ, MIRPAŚ); three occur only in moral and cultic contexts (GAʿAL, ṬAME, KATAM), and ŠIQQUṢ, GILLUL, PIGGUL denote the consequences of uncleanness rather than its nature. Later Hebrew MᵉLUKLAK 'dirty' is not attested in OT Hebrew, but this is probably an accident.[46] It would be equally risky to link the prominence of metallurgical terminology in the HOŠIAʿ-field with the 'Kenite hypothesis'.[47] On occasion some kind of correlation can be made: the fact that ṢEL, unlike its English equivalent 'shade, shadow', occurs in OT Hebrew only in the sense of protection (apart from the exceptional collocation with mawet 'death' in ṣalmawet 'the shadow of death'),[48] reflects climatic conditions in the Near East: cf.

Give counsel,
  grant justice;
make your shade like night
  at the height of noon;
hide the outcasts,
  betray not the fugitive . . . (Isa. 16.3)

But this is rare, and limited to rather obvious phenomena.

Few would dispute the claim of the field-theorists, however, that the size and structure of a field reflect to a very large extent the conditions of its historical context. The language of the OT, as we have seen, originated in various distinct contexts, and therefore no field which takes in the whole of OT Hebrew, could satisfactorily be used as a guide to any one historical situation. But there are some general historical observations that can be made on the size and structure of the HOŠIA'-field. They can conveniently be grouped under three headings: (1) 'Sperber's law', (2) cultic origins, and (3) the distinctiveness of OT Hebrew.

1. Hans Sperber argued that if at a certain time 'a complex of ideas is strongly charged with feeling', this will affect semantic development.[49] In the OT, ideas connected with divine intervention are clearly a case in point, and the size and richness of the HOŠIA'-field provide an obvious example of the influence of thought on language. A rough comparison between the field in OT Hebrew and the same field in later Hebrew bears this out.[50] It might be suggested that the size of the field in OT Hebrew is simply due to the exigencies of Hebrew poetic structure,[51] were it not for three other areas of semantic development which must also be put down to the effective operation of 'Sperber's law'.

The first is metaphorical transference which is peculiarly frequent in the HOŠIA'-field.[52] Thus, for example, not only do the words ROMEM, HERIM, etc. 'to raise up' occur in a metaphorical sense, as in English 'exalt', 'uplift', etc., but so also do two terms of more restricted application, HIMŠA and DILLA 'to draw water from a well', e.g.

He reached from on high, he took me,
    he drew me out of many waters;
He delivered me from my strong enemy. (II Sam. 22.17)[53]

Secondly, there are many examples of extension of meaning in the case of words collocated with YHWH: e.g. ZAKAR 'to remember', ŠAPAṬ, 'to judge', RAPA' 'to heal', ḤIYYA 'to give life to'.[54] Thirdly, there are cases of semantic borrowing that may also be the result of this consistent preoccupation of religious writers with the subject of divine intervention: e.g. PAṢA and PARAQ in the sense of 'to save' are probably two examples of borrowing from Aramaic in the very centre of the field.[55] ŠEMEŠ 'sun', applied to God in Ps. 84.12, is probably another example.[56] All these developments, metaphorical transference, extension of meaning and semantic borrowing, naturally affect the size of the HOŠIA'-field.

Not only the size of the field can be shown to have been influenced by historical factors, however; its structure also shows signs of similar developments. One case of this has already been mentioned, namely the peculiar productiveness of forensic terminology in language about salvation. A more precisely traceable example has been suggested in an examination of the 'spaciousness' sector. Almost all the passages in which language about salvation includes words for 'to give room to', 'spacious', etc. can reasonably be dated to periods of territorial expansion in Israel.[57] In other words, when the extension of Israel's political boundaries was 'in the news', language about divine intervention on behalf of Israel, or on behalf of individuals living in Israel, developed accordingly. Thus on the one hand the language of God's ancient promise of land is coloured by details of David's spectacular territorial gains (cf. Gen. 15.18ff.; Deut. 11.24; Josh. 1.4; etc.); while on the other hand the language of a psalm of thanksgiving after an individual's escape from danger contains some impressive new imagery: e.g.

> They came upon me in the day of my calamity;
>   but the Lord was my stay.
> He brought me forth into a broad place;
>   he delivered me, because he delighted in me.
>   (II Sam. 22.19f., cf. v.37)

A third example of the influence of historical events on the structure of the field may be found in the 'leading' sector. Here the deep impression made on the language of the OT by the Exodus events is perhaps reflected in the prominence of metaphors of leading and guiding, not only in contexts of intellectual or moral guidance, as in English, but also in situations of physical danger and distress: e.g.

> Yea, thou art my rock and my fortress;

for thy name's sake lead me and guide me,
take me out of the net which is hidden for me,
for thou art my refuge. (Ps. 31.3f.)

The prototype of divine intervention, as recorded in ancient poetry (e.g. Ex. 15.13) and confessional statements (e.g. Deut. 26.5-9; Josh. 24.2ff.), has left its mark on the idiom of the Hebrew language.

2. A different explanation of the origins of Hebrew idiom centres on the importance of the cult as a formative influence. Expressions which at a later stage of the development of Hebrew may have been metaphorical, were originally literal references to episodes in liturgical ceremonies and dramas. This theory is implied in discussions of the spiritualizing of cultic language: two well-known examples are the call addressed to YHWH 'Arise!' and the formulae which speak of the 'face of YHWH'. Another case is the spiritualized language of the 'confessions of Jeremiah', certainly related to the (cultic) psalms of lamentation.[58]

A specific ritual act seems to lie behind several expressions which belong to the HOŠIA'-field. 'Thou dost hold my right hand' (Ps. 73.23) can be traced to a well-attested feature of ancient Near Eastern ritual, as Gressmann showed forty years ago.[59] Behind the phrase 'gates of righteousness' (Ps. 118.19) probably lies a reference to the names given to the gates of the temple, as was the custom in ancient Babylon.[60] Neither expression need, however, be restricted to its literal cultic application.

More problematical are such graphic images as 'He set me secure on the heights' (Ps. 18.33b) and 'He will set me high upon a rock' (Ps. 27.5c). Do these have their origin in specific dramatic episodes? The cultic background of expressions like 'I gave my back to the smiters and my cheeks to those who pulled out the beard' (Isa. 50.6), as attested in Akkadian ritual texts, makes this a plausible hypothesis.[61] Many other expressions can, with little imagination, be explained in terms of elaborate representation in liturgical dramas: 'lifter up of my head' (Ps. 3.3, cf. 110.7); 'He will conceal me under the cover of his tent' (Ps. 27.5b); 'The Lord my God lightens my darkness' (Ps.

18.29; EVV 18.28); 'Take hold of shield and buckler, and rise for my help' (Ps. 35.2).

3. There is however a third possible explanation of the rich structure of the HOŠIA'-field in OT Hebrew. This involves a distinctive combination of both the factors already discussed, not only the overwhelming preoccupation of OT writers with the subject of God's intervention on behalf of his people (cf. Sperber's theory), but also the persistent and formative influence on their language of ancient Near Eastern cultic practice. Just how much common Near Eastern ritual was practised in ancient Israel at any one time is obscure, but it is now certain that at any rate the language associated with it played an important role in the development of OT Hebrew.[62] Indeed it is almost true to say that all the basic literary forms and motifs can be traced back to origins among Israel's neighbours. A recent study entitled *History and the Gods* illustrates how even Israel's presentation of historical events as divine manifestations was by no means unique in the ancient Near East. As the author of the monograph points out, this does not mean that there was nothing distinctive in views of history; but the distinctiveness is a matter of degree rather than of kind.[63]

This is precisely what our examination of OT language about divine intervention reveals. While Israel undoubtedly shared many beliefs and much cultic practice with their neighbours, the degree to which their language about divine intervention was developed (by metaphorical transference, extension of meaning, semantic borrowing, and the like), is a measure of the distinctiveness of the religion of Israel. It is the highly developed language in which historical events are represented as acts of divine intervention that is distinctive, whether or not this language originally reflected cultic practice. Two examples will illustrate how it appears that language about cultic institutions can develop so elaborately that the original connexion with the cult is snapped.

The first is the phrase 'my cup overflows' (Ps. 23.5). There seems little doubt that this motif of the cup originated in cultic practice, probably in connexion with its use as a means of divination; and that the opposition between 'cup of salvation' (e.g. Ps. 116.13) and 'cup of wrath' (e.g. Isa. 51.17,22; Lam.

4.21) reflects the two kinds of oracular answer possible. The distinctive development here is that the auspicious possibility, 'cup of salvation', has been elaborated so richly that any reference to actual divinatory procedure is obscure, and it becomes irrelevant whether lecanomancy was practised in Israel at the time or not.[64]

The second example is the undoubted cultic reference in Ps. 24.3:

> Who shall ascend the hill of the Lord?
> And who shall stand in his holy place?[65]

Again we cannot claim to know much about the original cultic practice associated with this, but the gap in our knowledge appears less important when we realize that there are many phrases like 'He will set me high upon a rock' (Ps. 27.5), 'Lead thou me to the rock that is higher than I' (Ps. 61.3; EVV 61.2), in which we are dealing less with references to specific ritual or historical situations than with what may be imaginative elaborations of an original cultic scene. It is in this highly developed elaboration of the stereotyped language of the cult that we should look for Israel's distinctive contribution to ancient Near Eastern soteriology. It is this language, developed in situations where faith in and speculation about acts of divine intervention were lively and creative to a unique degree, that has been the basis of the theology and liturgy of all the religious communities which accept the OT as their Bible, or as part of their Bible.

One of the most fascinating results of the field approach to the study of the OT, is that it provides illuminating cross-sections of OT language about particular subjects, in this case, 'salvation'. It would be something short of the truth to claim that this is an entirely adequate method of discovering 'all that the OT teaches' about salvation. But in comparison with other methods, as illustrated for example in *TDNT* and a number of well-respected 'concept-studies', which are confined to the examination of one word and the passages in which it happens to occur,[66] it represents a considerable step forward. It would also be dangerous to claim that the HOŠIA'-field is somehow co-extensive with the 'OT concept of salvation'. The advantage of this approach is a practical one: it provides a useful method of amassing and classifying all the relevant passages. The following are several illustrations of the kind of theological data obtainable from the HOŠIA‘-field, data which are seldom mentioned in studies on OT soteriology.[67]

One feature of the field, which has already been discussed as evidence for the distinctive prominence of ideas about salvation in the OT, is its size. We need only add here that salvation from every type of danger and distress, physical, spiritual and psychological, is described in the richest language in almost every literary genre in the OT. There is a further point immediately evident from a look at the passages represented in the HOŠIA‘-field: the writers almost invariably attribute their escapes and victories to divine intervention. One of the distinctive features of the term HOŠIA‘ itself is that it is almost never used with a subject other than YHWH or his appointed leaders.[68]

The interpretation of historical events as acts of divine intervention leads to three developments, nicely illustrated in the HOŠIA‘-field. First the language of metal-working adds an important theme to OT soteriology. Defeat, suffering and humiliation are compared to impurity in metal: e.g.

> How the gold has grown dim,
> how the pure gold has changed. (Lam. 4.1)[69]

The reference here is to the destruction of Jerusalem. But by an act of faith this situation can be transformed into ‘the furnace of affliction’ (Isa. 48.10),[70] whereby Jerusalem can be purified and refined: e.g.

> I will turn my hand against you
> and will smelt away your dross as with lye,
> and remove all your alloy . . .
> Afterwards you shall be called the city of righteousness,
> the faithful city. (Isa. 1.25f.)

The ultimate stage in this refining process may be death, and this too, in the eyes of the faithful martyrs, can be an act of salvation: e.g.

> . . . and some of those who are wise shall fall, to refine and to cleanse them and to make them white. (Dan. 11.35)[71]

A second development is a pessimistic corollary of the first.

Just as faith can transform tragedy into hope for the future, so scepticism in time of crisis can transform the utterances of faith into cynical parodies of traditional theology. A famous example is the strident 'misuse' of the phrase 'thou watcher of men', which usually refers to God's fatherly care and protection (e.g. Isa. 27.3; Ps. 12.8), to denote the warder of a hellish prison (Job 7.20).[72] Military imagery is used to describe moral and psychological help: e.g.

> Thou art my hiding-place and my shield;
> I hope in thy word. (Ps. 119.114)

'His angel encamps round about them' (Ps. 34.6); but in the tortured mind of Job, defence can be a claustrophobic experience far removed from salvation: e.g.

> His troops come together;
> they have cast up siegeworks against me,
> and encamp round about my tent. (Job 19.12)

Related to this development are the prophets' free variations on traditional themes. Joel's parody of a 'floating oracle' is well-known (4.10; EVV 3.10). Perhaps the opening of the book of Amos is another example: instead of the comforting words of the original oracle (Isa. 2.3; Micah 4.2), we read,

> The Lord will roar from Zion,
> and thunder from Jerusalem. (Amos 1.2)[73]

The last general theological observation that might be made here concerns the application of numerous expressions for physical health and political prosperity to moral or spiritual conditions. It would appear that there often is in OT Hebrew no clear distinction between terms describing physical and psychological conditions: for example, KOAḤ, ḤAYIL and ḤOZEQ can apply equally to moral and material strength. Words like K^{e}'EB 'pain', RAPA' 'to heal', and '^{a}RUKA 'the new tissue that grows over a healed wound' primarily belong to the physical sphere, but can be transferred to psychological contexts.[74] This has important consequences for OT translation and exegesis, and one well-known example will make this clear. The description of the 'suffering servant' in Isaiah 53 is couched in the language of physical disease and pain, but this does not preclude spiritual or mental interpretations. Just as Job's boils are merely a graphic, repulsive way of describing all suffering, for the purposes of the argument, so all suffering known to the audience of Isaiah, political oppression, injustice, guilt, home-sickness, humiliation, are involved in the suffering of the servant and therefore included in the act of divine intervention which heals and vindicates him in the end.[75] It is in translation that the problem is most acute: translators and commentators frequently lose the effect of the metaphor by introducing psychological terms, for example, 'griefs' and 'sorrows' (Isa. 53.3), which might sound inconsistent with the rest of the picture: 'wounded for our transgressions', 'bruised for our iniquities', 'his stripes' and the general repulsive physical appearance of the man.[76] When it is realized that in presenting a consistent, graphic picture of physical suffering, the author intended to depict, metaphorically, the nadir of degradation and desolation, including the plight of his audience, then translation is simpler and the meaning of the song a good deal plainer. The identity of the servant is then less important than his function, and the applicability of the poem to all suffering facilitated.[77]

These three observations, like the rest of this chapter, are intended to do no more than indicate the direction in which studies based on the HOŠIAʿ-field might move.

2. *Semantic Structure*

Every linguistic unit, from a single lexical item like HOŠIAʿ to a sentence or a longer utterance, as well as having a phonological and grammatical structure, also has a semantic structure. In the present study, we have again narrowed our terms of reference, quite arbitrarily, to focus primarily on semantic structure. The phonological structure of HOŠIAʿ and a possible connexion with Arabic wasiʿa has been where previous semantic discussions of this term have begun; and semantic description taking the morpheme as a basic unit is also possible, as Jenni's exhaustive study of *Das hebräische Piʿel,* and discussions of the root-morpheme in Semitic languages have shown.[78] But here, partly because semantic structure (at any rate under that name) is a relatively novel approach to the Hebrew lexicon, and partly because it is, in the last resort, the most important, a selection of structural phenomena applicable to any language will now be discussed with illustrations taken mainly from the HOŠIA‘-field.[79]

1. *Semantic motivation* provides a valuable criterion for establishing significant oppositions.[80] A word is said to be phonetically motivated when there is a direct correspondence between the sound and the sense: e.g. English ‘bang’, ‘zoom’ (as opposed to ‘sound’, ‘voice’). In the nature of the associative field under discussion here, we should not expect to find examples of this type. Morphological motivation occurs when a word is composed of independently intelligible components: e.g. ‘ash-tray’, ‘redhead’, as opposed to French *cendrier, blonde.* The third type of motivation occurs when a word is used in a transferred meaning, made possible by some similarity or analogy between its concrete meaning and the abstract phenomenon to which it is applied: e.g. ‘the root of evil’, ‘the fruits of peace’, koba‘ y^{e}šu‘a ‘the helmet of salvation’, ḥeble mawet ‘the bonds of death’. The term ‘transparent’ is applied to words motivated in any one of these three ways, over against ‘opaque’ words, which have no motivation.

Transparency is often a historical matter: for example, English ‘lord’ was once morphologically motivated *(hlaf-ward)*, but, after phonetic developments, has become opaque; HOŠIA‘ may once have been semantically motivated, if it was ever related to a word meaning ‘to be wide, spacious’. Since such a ‘relation’ is no longer evident, the word is opaque.[81]

There is furthermore a subjective element in this transparent/opaque distinction: a writer who is a linguist, or at least has a lively interest in comparative philology, may exploit an etymological motivation for a word, which would be unknown to most of his readers: modern scientific terms like ‘hypodermic’ and ‘necrophile’ are only transparent for someone who knows some Greek. In the writings of Al Ḥariri, to quote an example from Arabic literature, special use is made of etymological motivation, in order to fascinate and intrigue the informed reader. Some definition of the style must therefore precede any statements about the transparency or opaqueness of certain words. But broadly speaking, in spite of these two provisos, the distinction is helpful and the terminology valuable.

It has been suggested elsewhere that in Hebrew a distinctive type of morphological motivation operates, due to the structure of the language.[82] The relatively small number of morphological patterns, the remarkable stability of the triconsonantal root, the consonantal script, and the frequency of folk-etymologies in OT Hebrew, have been adduced as reasons for supposing that in Hebrew we may have to take account of a type of etymological motivation (or at any rate 'folk-etymological' motivation) more developed than in the Indo-European languages. A 'root-meaning', in other words, may produce a kind of transparency. Words containing the same root often seem to contain an obvious semantic element in common, and an interesting example of this is provided by three Hebrew words for 'true/truth': ᵓᵉMET, NAKON YAṢṢIB. The three roots involved, *'MN, *KWN and *NṢB, also appear in words for 'to establish' and 'pillar', thus exhibiting a recurring semantic element in all three word-groups. Naturally this too is affected by historical factors. Often the development has gone a good deal further than this, so that the semantic connexion between a word and its root has virtually snapped: this is what has happened in later Hebrew examples like ṣᵉdaqa 'almsgiving' and NASAʿ 'to travel', words which earlier denoted 'righteousness' and 'to pull out a tent-peg' respectively. But this does not alter the fact that in the corpus of the OT, root and (synchronic) meaning are frequently closeley related. There is thus evidence for a peculiar kind of etymological motivation in OT Hebrew. Whether this means that Hebrew is to be considered a 'highly motivated language', like Sanskrit or German as opposed to Chinese which represents an extreme form of opaqueness, depends on whether some statistical test can be devised with which to compare it with these other languages.[83]

2. A second useful distinction is that between *general* and *particular terms*. Examples are easy to find in many languages: the general term *aller* in French corresponds to three particular terms in German, *gehen*, 'to walk', *reiten* 'to ride' and *fahren* 'to drive', and two in modern Hebrew, namely HALAK, 'to go (on foot)' and NASAʿ 'to go (by car, train, etc.)'. In contrast to

English 'open' which is a general term, the semantic spread of Hebrew PATAḤ 'to open' is limited by the co-presence of a number of particular terms: PAQAḤ 'to open (eyes, ears)', PAṢA 'to open (mouth)' PA'AR 'to open (mouth; in modern Hebrew, to undress for defecation)'. Similarly, in contrast to the general term 'to put on' in English, the semantic spread of Hebrew LABAŠ 'to put on (clothes, vestments)' is limited by the co-presence of NA'AL 'to put on (sandals)', ḤAGAR 'to put on (a sword)', 'AṬA 'to put on (cloak, veil)', ŚIM 'to put on (ornaments)'.

3. *Polysemy* is the name given to the use of the same word in two or more distinct senses in such a way as to produce, in effect, two separate words. It is caused by the parallel development of two applications of a word, for example, a concrete application and an abstract one, or the original one and a metaphorical one, until the connexion between the two snaps, resulting in two distinct words of identical form. The most frequently quoted examples are English 'pupil (of the eye)' alongside 'pupil (at school)', and French *voler* 'to fly' alongside *voler* 'to steal'. In both these cases there is enough historical evidence to prove that the two pairs were originally connected.

The distinction between polysemy and *homonymy* depends on historical factors: if it were proved that *voler* 'to fly' and *voler* 'to steal' were historically distinct, this would be an example of homonymy. Homonyms are due to phonetic developments which make two originally quite distinct lexical items converge. We are not concerned with aural examples (e.g. French *cinq, ceint, sain, sein, saint;* English 'meat', 'meet'), since we are dealing with written texts. The nature of the consonantal script has resulted in a peculiar kind of 'visual homonymy': for example, D-B-R, unpronounced, can be dabar 'word, thing', dibber 'he spoke', dubbar 'it was spoken', dabber 'speak', deber 'plague', d^{e}bir 'inner sanctuary'. The semantics of unpointed Hebrew would probably provide a fascinating and rewarding subject for a doctoral dissertation, and H.B. Rosén has written on the process of identifying Hebrew words in unpointed texts, for the benefit of students whose intuitive knowledge of Hebrew is as yet elementary.[84] In this present study we are concerned with the masoretic text only, and these problems do not arise.

Polysemy and homonymy inevitably produce ambiguity, and subsequent 'therapeutic' processes and safeguards emerge.[85] Orthographic safeguards are frequent: e.g. English 'draft' beside 'draught'; Hebrew QARA' 'to read' beside QARA 'to meet' (the process is not complete in this example before Mishnaic Hebrew), NAŠA' 'to beguile' beside NAŠA 'to lend'. Morphological safeguards exist too: for instance I. GA'AL 'to act as a kinsman' and II. GA'AL 'to stain' are not homonyms in Biblical Hebrew, although the arrangement in BDB makes them look as if they are. In reality the two words are GA' AL (Qal) 'to act as a kinsman' and GE'AL (Piel) 'to stain'. Similar distinctions are evident for PARAQ (Qal) 'to rescue' beside PEREQ (Piel) 'to tear apart'; and ḤALAṢ (Qal) 'to take off, strip' beside ḤILLEṢ (Piel) 'to rescue'. Thirdly, contextual factors cut down ambiguity still further, and it is remarkable how few examples of either polysemy or homonymy actually produce ambiguity in OT Hebrew, especially when one considers the nature of the script, the phonemes that have converged in Hebrew, and the relatively limited number of morphological patterns.

On account of our slender evidence for the prehistory of Biblical Hebrew, it is often hard to distinguish examples of homonymy and polysemy, one from the other. The tendency in traditional OT lexicography is to assume that two semantically distinct words of identical form are homonyms, and to prove this by reference to comparative philology. This can be misleading: for instance, in the two standard lexica there are four entries under the form ʿANA: I. 'to answer, testify'; II. 'to be downcast'; III. 'to be worried'; IV. 'to sing'. The distinction between I and IV is based, on the one hand, on English translation and, on the other, on comparative etymology. But this is not supported by the evidence: (1) both occur in similar contexts, both cultic (e.g. Deut. 21.7; 26.51 (I), and Ex. 32.18 (IV)); and general (e.g. Num. 11.28; Judg. 18.14 (I) and I Sam. 18.7; 21.12 (IV); (2) the translations which distinguish them most clearly ('to answer' and 'to sing') are not adequate in every context, e.g. Gen. 30.33 (I) 'to testify'; Jer. 25.30 (IV) 'to shout'; and (3) there is sometimes doubt as to which is meant (e.g. Hos. 2.17).[86] When we add (4) the etymological evidence of Ugaritic m'nh 'its (liturgical) response' and Syriac 'ANI 'to sing responsively',[87] there hardly seems to be any good reason left for distinguishing etymologically between I and IV. With this background for 'ANA in biblical Hebrew, passages like Hos. 2.17,24, and Jer. 25.30 are more easily understood, even although translation still remains a problem. I. 'ANA and IV. 'ANA are probably examples of polysemy, not homonymy.

4. When an expression is taken from one sphere and applied in a totally different one because of similarities of various kinds, this process is described as *metaphorical transference*. It is common in many languages, and results in a number of semantically motivated words and expressions like 'the brow of the hill', 'the family-tree', 'scintillating wit', 'a piercing cry', and so on.

Anthropomorphic metaphors are frequent in Hebrew as elsewhere: ro'š hassela' '(lit.) the head of the rock', ragle harim '(lit.) the feet of the mountains', yad wašem 'a monument (lit. hand) and a name'. It should be noted that in theological language the term anthropomorphism is used, in a restricted sense, for the application of human attributes to God. In the OT this varies from the crude anthropomorphism of Gen. 3 to the exalted imagery of Isa. 40-55. [88] Most language about God is anthropomorphic: but there is one interesting peculiarity about OT Hebrew which perhaps distinguishes it from other languages. Certain words are applied only to God, and never in human contexts. The best known of these is BARA' 'to create'; but HOŠIA' is another example of a word primarily reserved for the activity of God. In English 'to create' and 'to save' can be applied respectively in contexts of an artist's work and housekeeping; this is never found in OT Hebrew, and indeed is specifically forbidden.[89] The phenomenon is undoubtedly due to the nature of the texts and the theological interests of the writers. Again it seems likely that originally these words had a wider application. But the process of 'disinfecting' words to avoid any kind of anthropomorphism is complete at least in the case of BARA' and almost complete in the case of HOŠIA'.

Another frequent type of metaphorical transference is from concrete to abstract: e.g. English 'to befog', 'on top of the world', 'to let down', 'the way of truth'; Hebrew ha'am hahol^e kim bahošek 'the people that walk in darkness', ṣur 'uzzi 'the rock of my strength', etc. There is a very large number of metaphorical transfers of this type in the HOŠIA'-field, which provide a convenient means of classifying many of the items in it. Metaphorical transference from concrete to abstract is more common than the opposite type.[90]

The theory already discussed that if at a certain time 'a complex of ideas is strongly charged with feeling' this will affect various linguistic processes,[91] applies particularly to metaphorical transference: for example, *atomique* became the colloquial French term of enthusiastic approbation at a time when atomic energy was in the news, and German and modern Hebrew *Eisenbeton* when prestressed concrete was discovered. In the HOŠIA'-field there is one very noticeable example of this, namely metaphorical transference from the legal sphere: PADA, GA'AL, ŠAPAṬ, DIN, RIB, PAQAD, ṢEDEQ are some examples. Indeed it is almost true to say that there are no forensic terms which do not appear in this field. The most crucial of all is the basic metaphor for the relationship of Israel to their God, namely the legal contract contained in the word b^e rit 'covenant'. The immediate importance of this observation for our analysis of the meaning of HOŠIA', is that it lends some support to the suggestion that it too was originally a forensic term.[92]

This theory would also help to explain the size of the HOŠIA'-field, particularly in the register we have selected. It would not require much research to prove that the complex of ideas associated with the word HOŠIA' was 'strongly charged with feeling' for OT writers, and the result is metaphorical transference from almost every sphere of human experience: light, space, height, medicine, war, washing, building, leading and others.[93]

5. Examples of the processes of *extension and restriction of meaning* are frequent in Hebrew as in other languages. An interesting one is DABAR, which seems to have been limited originally to 'the spoken word', and later extended, or weakened to 'thing', just as Latin *causa* is weakened to Italian *cosa* 'thing', and Old English *thing* 'parliament' to modern English 'thing'. The effect of this on the vocabulary of the OT is

that an Aramaic loan-word milla came to be used for 'word', except in a number of petrified phrases like d^e bar YHWH 'the word of the Lord'. Legal terminology like GA'AL 'to redeem', PADA 'to ransom', ŠAPAṬ 'to judge' and ṢEDEQ 'justice' have been extended in application to non-technical contexts. HOŠIA' may be an example of an extension of meaning so complete that traces of its original, technical application are rare in OT Hebrew.[94]

Modern Greek *ψωμί* 'bread' and *ψάρι* 'fish' are good examples of restriction of meaning, from classical Greek *ὄψωμα* 'morsel, bit' and *ὀψάριον* diminutives of *ὄψος* 'anything eaten with bread'. English 'fowl', 'beef' and 'mutton' illustrate a similar process, over against German *Vogel*, French *boeuf* and *mouton*. Hebrew participial forms like ŠOMER, ḤOZE, ŠOPEṬ, MAZKIR, are to be considered as examples of restriction of meaning from 'one who keeps', 'one who sees, judges, reminds' to a technical sense 'watchman', 'seer', 'judge', 'secretary'.

A slightly different type of restriction has been referred to already, namely the reservation of certain words for a specifically theological context: BARA' 'to create' (only with God as subject), HOŠIA' 'to save' (almost exclusively with God or his appointed servant as subject).

6. *Lexical borrowing* in the OT has been dealt with up till now mainly from the point of view of loanwords, classified according to the source-language. There have been several studies like 'Hittite Words in Hebrew' (Rabin), 'Indo-European Words in Hebrew' (Rabin), and *Die lexikalischen und grammatikalischen Aramäismen im alttestamentlichen Hebräisch* (M. Wagner).[95] But there have been no studies in OT Hebrew comparable with that of T.E. Hope on 'Loanwords as Cultural and Lexical Symbols' in French.[96] This is not the place to undertake such a task. But it would be valuable to enumerate some factors operating in lexical borrowing in OT Hebrew.

The most obvious cause is a gap in the vocabulary: sus 'horse' was required when Hebrew speakers came first into contact with Indo-European horse-breeders: the same is true of the Greek words for the musical instruments like psanter, sumponia (Dan. 3.5). In the HOŠIA'-field there are two examples of borrowing from Aramaic: PARAQ 'to tear apart' (Hebrew), 'to rescue' (Aramaic); and PAṢA 'to open' (Hebrew), 'to rescue' (Aramaic). The occurrence of a parallel development like this suggests a common cause. In this case borrowing could be attributed either to the exigencies of Hebrew verse-form, which demanded many 'synonymous parallels', or the lively interest of the OT writers in this particular subject. Incidentally, borrowing in this field also occurs in Samaritan Aramaic ʾOŠIAʿ 'to save'.

A fourth factor might be the artificial introduction of an aetiological loan-word by one whose native language was not Hebrew, for exegetical purposes. One example of this seems to be the folk-etymology of the name Japheth in Gen. 9.27: 'God enlarge Japheth'. PETI 'simple', and PITTA 'to deceive' occur in Hebrew, but PATI 'to be wide, spacious' occurs only in Aramaic. A similar explanation for the folk-etymology of the name Abraham (Gen. 17.5) is likely, and also of YHWH (Ex. 3.14).[97]

Finally there is the effect of a dominating religious, cultural or political environment. OT examples of this are HEKAL (from Sumerian E-GAL) 'temple, palace', and Aramaic DAT (from Old Persian *datam*) 'law'.

Borrowing can be conveniently examined in terms of lexical fields: changes in the size of a field, convergence and divergence of related words, and other historical developments provide a promising approach to the problem of defining loanwords and semantic borrowings. Again the historical fact that a word in OT Hebrew is a loanword may have little or nothing to do with its meaning, synchronically: modern Hebrew dati 'religious', for example, would best be defined without reference to its Old Persian origins.

7. *Taboo* has a number of linguistic consequences which can be observed in many languages. Taboo subjects may be classified broadly into three groups: those inspired by a religious fear (Freud's 'holy dread'), those due to a sense of delicacy, and those due to a sense of decency. Examples of the first would include the well-known substitutions in OT Hebrew for the names of gods: e.g. bošet 'abomination' for Baal in Ishbosheth and elsewhere;[98] ʾadonai 'the Lord', haššem 'the Name', hašša-

mayim 'Heaven' and the like for the unpronounceable tetragrammaton YHWH. A similar development occurs in modern English 'Heaven help us!' and 'Goodness knows!'

Taboo subjects in most languages, like sex, certain parts of the body and bodily functions, have produced euphemisms in Hebrew as elsewhere: e.g. raglayim 'private parts', BOʾ ʾEL 'to come in to', ŠAKAB ʿIM 'to lie with', YADAʿ 'to know' are all euphemisms for sexual intercourse. It should be noted that these are regular developments due to taboo, and tell us nothing of the meaning of the euphemistic terms: to argue that there is some special meaning in YADAʿ because it is used as a euphemism for sexual intercourse,[99] is no more convincing than it would be to suggest that modern colloquial English 'to have' has some special meaning since it is applied in a similar taboo context. Euphemistic terms are often selected just because they are neutral words and of general application.

8. One of the most common linguistic phenomena adduced to explain semantic change is *analogy*. At all levels, phonological, grammatical and lexical, there is 'interference'[100] in the development of words, due to their association with other words of related meaning. In Hebrew the form ḥᵃmišša 'five' is due to its close relationship with šišša 'six'.[101]

An important case of interference which concerns the semantic description of a number of words in the HOŠIAʿ-field, has confused commentators and resulted in semantic and textual fabrication. In Ps. 43.1 we have the following construction:

riba ribi miggoy loʾ ḥasid
defend my cause (lit.) from an ungodly people.

The translators have had to render the prepositional adjunct 'against an ungodly people' (RSV; cf. AV), although it is understood that the phrase is really 'pregnant (so as to rescue from)'.[102] The difficulty can best be explained with reference to the field in which the word RIB occurs. By its regular association with HOŠIAʿ, HIṢṢIL, PADA, GAʾAL, etc., all of which are regularly followed by min- 'from', RIB has been affected in such a way as to admit of a similar construction. ŠAPAṬ 'to judge' behaves in exactly the same way, and must be rendered in English by some kind of periphrasis: e.g. 'vindicate (by rescuing) from the hand of'. It occurs in contexts exactly parallel to HOŠIA'.[103] Seen against the background of their associative field, these two verbs demonstrate a natural semantic development.

There is a third forensic term which has probably undergone the same development, due to its association with HOŠIA', HIṢṢIL, etc.:

> haṣṣila miḥereb napši
>   miyyad keleb y^{e}ḥidati
> hoši'eni mippi 'arie
> umiqqarne remim '^{a}nitani. (Ps. 22.21f.; EVV 22.20f.)

Three members of the HOŠIA'-field occur in this verse and are all followed by min- 'from'. Of these, two (HOŠIA' and HIṢṢIL) are regularly followed by min- 'from', but the third 'ANA is nowhere else accompanied by this preposition. The problem has produced two main solutions: (1) emend the text to 'aniyyati 'my afflicted soul'; (2) take umiqqarne remim with the preceding hoši'eni, and '^{a}nitani as an independent cry concluding the *Klagelied* 'Thou hast heard me'.[104] Seen against the background of its associative field, however, the word raises no problem (except perhaps for the translator). Like ŠAPAṬ and RIB, 'ANA is a forensic term, 'to speak up as a witness, to testify'; and like these other two terms, its frequent association with HOŠIA', HIṢṢIL, etc., has affected it both semantically and syntactically: 'You have defended me from the horns of the wild oxen'.[105]

9. *Semantic components* (or 'markers') enable us to make general statements about groups of words which obviously have something in common: e.g. 'man', 'bull', 'stallion', 'cock' have in common the semantic components (Male) and (Adult), as opposed to the group 'woman', 'cow', 'mare', 'hen' which have the components (Female) and (Adult) in common.[106] Without entering into the debate as to whether these 'semantic components' are part of the cognitive structure of the human mind, or whether the meaning of more complex terms will ever be adequately defined in terms of the sum total of their semantic components, one would expect the notion to be a helpful one in the study of a group of related words like the

present. For example, is it significant that of the six commonest words in the HOŠIA' group, only one, 'AZAR, is a Qal form? This is a grammatical 'component' which most of the group have in common; is it also a semantic component? Jenni's study on *Das hebräische Pi'el* suggests that all Piel forms in OT Hebrew do have a semantic element in common.[107] An important 'element of separation' is also observable in the verbs of the HOŠIA'-group,[108] an element which has had semantic influence on related terms: this might well be described as a semantic component. But in that case we would have to allow for varying degrees of importance in some components, since this element is more prominent in HIṢṢIL, for example, than in HOŠIA' or 'AZAR, and also context-sensitive. Perhaps some other elements, such as 'root-meanings' and other types of semantic motivation, could be described as semantic components.

Componential analysis is more obviously applicable to some parts of the lexicon than others,[109] and there are immense problems still not finally solved. For example, it appears that labelling the components depends only on the linguist's intuitive knowledge rather than on some more objective criteria within the language, and it is to be doubted whether a means can be devised for distinguishing between 'mare' and 'nag' on componential terms, without reference to contextual criteria as well. But as a way of making semantics as objective and 'structural' a discipline as phonology, grammar and syntax, it is a promising beginning.[110]

IV

SYNCHRONIC DESCRIPTION

The reasons for selecting this particular lexical group for the investigation may be briefly set forth as follows. It is an interesting one on several accounts: it contains HOŠIAʿ, by far the most frequent item in the field and one which, in contrast to other items in the same field, like HIRḤIB 'to give room to' and ŚIGGEB 'to make high', for example, has no obvious metaphorical motivation.[1] Modern descriptions of the word have relied almost exclusively on etymological data, and a synchronic analysis from within the language would seem in this case to be especially promising. It would also be true to say that the usual English equivalents, 'to save', 'salvation', 'saviour', have tended to obscure the meaning of HOŠIAʿ, by their very wide application in religious contexts. The same holds for HIṢṢIL and ʿAZAR. The distinction between these three and the other words in the sector has not yet been systematically defined, and it is the aim of this analysis to define and distinguish these closely related words.

Naturally the meaning of these words is familiar to a greater or lesser extent to anyone who knows Hebrew, and it may be that this analysis will discover nothing new. But in that case it is hoped that previous intuitive ideas can be given a more objective basis in accordance with sound linguistic theory.[2] As we shall see, the agreement between several of the results and 'what is generally believed' about the words is striking: for example, the stylistic difference between HOŠIAʿ and ʿAZAR, the secular use of the latter, and the element of separation apparent especially in HIṢṢIL. This would suggest two possibilities: (1) there is some truth in the conclusions if they can be arrived at from two quite different angles; (2) what is true of the register in particular is also true of the whole OT. This second point can be further substantiated by a less detailed survey of the rest of the OT, which will be undertaken in Chapter V. But it must be emphasized that the narrow concentration on one section of OT language was not intended to provide a representative cross-section of the OT, although if it does incidentally this would be valuable. The selection of one register from within the OT (indeed one part of that register) was simply intended to cut down the relevant data to easily manageable proportions so that the main emphasis should be on the method of linguistic description, rather than on the completeness of the results.

1. *The Lexical Group HOŠIA', HIṢṢIL, etc.*

All the occurrences of HOŠIA', HIṢṢIL, etc. in the register were noted on paper-slips, grouped in the first instance according to style.[3] As one would expect, each of the members of the lexical group occurs in many different forms: for example, while the second person masculine singular forms of HOŠIA' are naturally most frequent in language addressed to God, passives, infinitives, imperatives and so on also occur. There are also the nominal forms YEŠA', Y^e ŠU'A, T^e ŠU'A. Now if, for convenience in classifying the data, we select the conventional citation-form (third person masculine singular of the perfect) as the form quoted in the analysis, we are confronted by a set of relations which require some explanation. In dealing with the word hoši'eni (Jer. 17.14) for instance, we may profitably speak of the occurrence of HOŠIA' in this context, and this is the generally accepted procedure, but in so doing we are assuming a relationship between hoši'eni and the citation form HOŠIA' which is not self-explanatory. Is it a grammatical relation? Or is it a semantic one, or an etymological one? When we bring in the nominal forms YEŠA', Y^e ŠU'A etc. as well, the problem is more complicated. What is the precise relation between HOŠIA' and NATAN T^e ŠU'A (cf. Judg. 15.18b)?

The most common method of describing this relation is by reference to etymology. Words derived from a common root are related to each other like members of a family or branches of a tree. This leads to the further assumption that words containing the same root share a common semantic element, and that therefore it is possible to extract and analyse the meaning of the root. The dangers of etymologizing are only too well known, and there is no need to enlarge on the subject here. It is enough to say that the semantic relation between a word and its root is an extremely complex one, even when, as in the case of *YŠʿ, the relation between the cognates is relatively simple. What is more, to take a root, which is by definition divorced from any context, as the subject of a semantic analysis, would be directly opposed to all we have said about the importance of dealing with language in context.

The alternative which is being proposed here is based on one of the most productive insights of modern linguistic theory, namely, transformational grammar.[4] This is not the place for any kind of detailed account of Chomskian linguistics, nor is the present writer qualified for such an undertaking. But this is an important field of modern linguistic theory which is comparatively little known among OT Hebrew linguists, and, in the present context, provides a valuable method of analysing all the heterogeneous material involved. The following brief introduction to that part of transformational grammar which concerns us has been included here.

Unlike traditional grammars, which are concerned with regularities discernible in the surface of a language, these new 'generative' grammars (transformational grammar in particular) describe the rules according to which all grammatical sentences in a language are generated from a deep structure or kernel. Chomsky himself believes that this deep structure is a reality underlying all natural languages, and inherent in the language faculty of the human species. Not all would agree with this; but interest in the way a perfectly structured sentence is generated, for example, by children who have never heard it before, is common to all generative grammars. They are concerned not so much with language, as with linguistic competence. They describe relations between surface structure and deep structure rather than relations between elements in the surface structure. Two related sentences provide examples:

(a) <u>hošiaʿ</u> <u>YHWH</u> <u>ʾet-mᵉšiḥo</u> 'the Lord saved his anointed' (Ps. 20.7; EVV 20.6).

(b) hosiʿeni 'save me' (Jer. 17.14).

These are ultimately derivable from one underlying structure, and transformational grammar describes the rules required to generate these two sentences from a common 'kernel': NP1 + V+NP2 (in both cases the first two terms are the same: YHWH and HOŠIAʿ). We shall not enumerate the rules required here, but it is clear that these would simply be matters of person, tense, mood and the like. We may take as an example a passive sentence:

(c) ʾiwwašeaʿ 'I shall be saved' (II Sam. 22.4).

This is generated from the same underlying structure by a similar set of fairly straightforward rules, and all three sentence-types, Active Declarative, Active Imperative and Passive Declarative can conveniently be cited as occurrences of HOŠIAʿ.[5] Then the (paradigmatic) relations between HOŠIAʿ and other terms in its environment (e.g. RAPAʾ in Jer. 17.14), and matters concerning, for example, transitivity, are clarified.[6]

The relation between HOŠIAʿ and the nominal forms yesaʿ, y^{e}šuʿa etc. can similarly be described in transformational terms. A sentence like the following can be said to have been generated from the same kernal as (a), (b) and (c) by a different set of rules, involving in this case a nominalization:

(d) ʾatta natatta ʾet-hatt^{e}šuʿa hagg^{e}dola hazzot b^{e}yad ʿabd^{e}ka
You have let your servant win this great victory (Judg. 15.18b).

Nominalization is the process whereby the verb HOŠIAʿ (translatable as 'gave victory', cf. Ps. 20.6 NEB) is rewritten as a noun or noun-phrase in the surface structure. Since it will prove to be of considerable significance as widening and enriching a term's semantic range, some more detailed remarks on this particular area of transformational grammar are necessary. Four general principles concerning nominalization in Hebrew may be formalized:

1. Nominalization normally involves the deletion of either the subject or the object of the verb. In the phrase y^{e}šuʿat

yiśra'el 'the salvation of Israel' (Ps. 14.7) the subject (YHWH probably) is deleted; in the phrase yᵉšuʿat YHWH 'the salvation of the Lord' (Ex. 14.13) the object (probably yiśra'el) is deleted. This makes a decision on whether an occurrence is transitive or intransitive difficult, and occasionally leads to ambiguity as in the phrase yᵉšuʿatka 'your salvation' (Gen. 49.18) in which the identity of the (deleted) object is unclear.[7] In English nominalization without deletion is common: e.g. 'the Lord's salvation of Israel'.

2. Nominalization normally involves deletion of the tense-marker as well. In the example just quoted from Gen. 49.18 not only is it unclear who or what the object of the saving act could be, but the tense is also obscure. RSV and NEB suggest an event in the future; according to JB the statement is of quite general application and holds good for all time. Other examples are ʾᵉlohe yišʿenu 'God of our salvation' (I Chron. 16.35) and ṣur yᵉšuʿatenu 'rock of our salvation' (Ps. 89.27). Tense is unmarked in such noun-phrases, and when these are analysed along the lines suggested here, the problem of tense inevitably arises. A well-known instance of this difficulty occurs in Isa. 53.5, where the noun-phrase musar šᵉlomenu 'the chastisement of our peace' (AV) has been variously translated in recent years as 'the chastisement designed for our peace', 'the chastisement that made us whole' and 'a punishment that brings us peace'.[8] The underlying structure of this phrase would therefore have to be reconstructed either without tense-markers or with alternatives. In practice however the tense of HOŠIAʿ in this type of nominalization rarely affects the semantic analysis, and is only really significant in some of the meaning-relations.[9]

3. When a nominalization is 'embedded' in a verbal sentence (which has its own, separate underlying kernel), the verb may be merely a 'function word' like PAʿAL (e.g. Ps. 74.12) or ʿAŚA (e.g. I Sam. 14.45). The distinction between a function word or 'empty word' and a 'full word' goes back to the nineteenth century,[10] and is a valuable one, although difficult to define precisely; 'there is a complete intergradation from items which are almost purely structural markers, to ones which have considerable lexical meaning'.[11] It is often a matter of context: in I Kings 8.34 natatta 'you have given (the land)' has 'considerable lexical meaning'. But in Judg. 15.18b, quoted above, it

is not easy to describe the distinction between natatta ʾet-hattᵉsuʿa 'you have given the victory' and hošaʿta 'you have given help' (e.g. Job 26.2). It seems reasonable to consider NATAN in the first example as an 'empty verb' or structural marker, required, like PAʿAL and ʿAŚA, by the nominalization rules.

A second example illustrates how, in place of an empty verb like NATAN or PAʿAL, a verb with some appropriate meaning may be introduced with the nominalization:

(e) kohᵃneka YHWH ʾᵉlohim yilbᵉšu tᵉšuʿa
May your priests, O Lord God, be clothed with salvation (II Chron. 6.41).

Here the verb corresponding to NATAN and PAʿAL is LABAŠ 'to wear vestments' which is obviously apt in this context. The underlying verbal structure which generated (a) above is rewritten, like (c), according to the appropriate rules, as a passive sentence (*yiwwašᵉu kohᵃneka), which is then embedded, according to the appropriate nominalization rules, in the sentence yilbᵉšu 'let them wear vestments'.[12]

4. This brings us to the last point we have to deal with in connexion with nominalization, namely, the generation of one sentence from a twofold underlying structure which could generate two separate sentences: e.g.

(f) lišuʿatka qiwwiti YHWH 'I wait for your salvation, O Lord' (Gen. 19.18).

Underlying this sentence are two kernel structures from which could be generated the two sentences *hošiaʿ YHWH ʾet-NP and qiwwiti lᵃYHWH.[13] Probably verbless sentences of the following type ought also to be included here:

(g) ʾatta ṣur yᵉšuʿati 'you are the rock of my salvation' (cf. Ps. 89.27).

The same kernel that underlies (a), (b) and (c) is embedded in the sentence ʾatta ṣuri 'you are my rock' (cf. Ps. 62.2).

In sentences of the type (f) and (g) it is not difficult to reconstruct the two separate sentences at least partially, even if both the object and tense-marker have been deleted according to the nominalization rules mentioned above. But in the remaining examples the analysis is a little more problematical. We begin with the question of the semantic distinction between the two following sentences:

A. wayᵉhi li lišuʿa 'and he has become my salvation' (Ex. 15.2).

B. wayyosaʿ li 'and he saved me' (cf. Ex. 14.30).

If HAYA in A is merely a function word, then there is virtually no difference in meaning between A and B. It seems possible, however, that there is a difference indicated by the verbless clauses ze ʾeli . . . ʾᵉlohe ʾabi 'He is my God . . . my father's God . . .' which come immediately after A. A lays more stress on the personal relationship between subject and object than B, a relationship which is elaborated in the rest of the verse. In transformational terms, a double structure underlies A which could generate two separate sentences, wayyošaʿ li (cf. Ex. 14.30) and a sentence of the type, *wayᵉhi YHWH ʾitti 'and the Lord was with me' (cf. Gen. 39.21).

The next example is hard to explain:

YHWH lᵉhošiʿeni (Isa. 38.20).

The suggestions *'wird mich retten' (tempus instans)* and 'is ready to save me' are little help since they could equally well be translations of the normal yosiʿeni (e.g. Ps. 55.17). Others emend the text.[14]

The last example illustrates how transformational analysis may uncover a new interpretation:

ʾaken bᵃ YHWH ʾᵉlohenu tᵉšuʿat yiśraʾel
Truly in the Lord our God is the salvation of Israel (Jer. 3.23).

What is the significance of the preposition bᵉ- here? According to the nominalization rules one would expect the preposition lᵉ- in this construction (cf. lᵃ YHWH hayᵉšuʿa, Ps. 3.9). bᵉ- rarely indicates the agent;[15] and in the only two instances where bᵃ YHWH occurs in this position; (Jer. 3.23: Deut. 33.29) the verb is HOSIAʿ. Every other occurence of bᵃ YHWH (83 times) is with verbs like BAṬAḤ 'to trust', HEʾᵉMIN 'to believe', SAMEAḤ 'to rejoice', ŠAʾAL 'to consult', and NIŠBAʿ 'to swear'. This suggests the possibility of interference between

HOŠIA' and, let us say, BAṬAḤ 'to trust', a term which is not infrequently associated in OT Hebrew.[16] The corresponding English sentences make this point clearer: 'Israel's trust is in the Lord' beside 'Israel's salvation is in the Lord'. Both in English and in Hebrew the preposition b^e 'in' could conceivably be locative (cf. Josh. 22.25,27), or else, in Hebrew, it might even be considered *beth essentiae* (cf. Ex. 6.3).[17] But neither of these solutions can be said to be more convincing than the one recommended here. Underlying the familiar sentence in Jer. 3.23 is a double structure from which two separate sentences could have been generated;

A. hošia' YHWH et-yiśra'el (cf. Ex. 14.30).
B. yiśra'el b^e ṭaḥ b^a YHWH (Ps. 115.9).

The noun-phrase t^e su'at yiśra'el 'the salvation of Israel', generated according to the nominalization rules from the same kernel as A, is then embedded in B. The prepositional verb BAṬAḤ b^e 'to trust in'[18] is only partially deleted, since b^a YHWH 'in the Lord', in opposition to laššeqer 'a delusion', in association with HOŠIA', and as it does in over 80 other passages, expresses the object of hope and trust.

The advantages of reducing all the occurrences of the root *YŠ' to a function of the verb HOŠIA' are obvious, and the same is true for the other terms under discussion. But it must be stressed that this is a grammatical device, and it would be misleading to suggest that, for example, NATAN T^e ŠU'A always 'means the same' as HOŠIA', or that LABAŠ Y^e ŠU'A is necessarily the passive of HOŠIA'. The transformational model implies some kind of semantic equivalence, but 'congruence between grammatical and semantic (transformational) structure' need not necessarily hold in every case.[19] The meaning of each item will be dealt with individually, each in its context.

1. HOŠIA' occurs 38 times in the register, in contrast to HIṢṢIL, 'AZAR, and PILLEṬ, which each occur only 7 times and ḤILLEṢ and PARAQ which each occur only once. MILLEṬ and PAṢA do not occur at all in the set-piece style.[20] This overwhelming predominance of HOŠIA' is too striking to be an accident due to the size of the sample, and is the first distinctive characteristic of the term over against the rest of the

group.

Secondly, a stylistic distinction can be drawn between ʿAZAR and the other terms. A glance at Table 1 will show this: while HOŠIAʿ, HIṢṢIL, PILLEṬ, ḤILLEṢ and PARAQ occur mainly in the same four styles (HITPALLEL, ṢAʿAQ, ŠIR), ʿAZAR occurs only once in any of these styles (Judg. 5.23, which is exceptional in other respects too), and most frequently in two styles in which HOŠIAʿ is comparatively rare and the others are not attested at all (QARAʾ, BEREK).[20] Again the consistency of this picture, even in a small sample, is remarkable, and provides us with a further distinction within the lexical group.

One other interesting distributional fact about HOŠIAʿ is that, with one exception, it is the only member of the group that occurs in the prophets: Isaiah (8 times), Jeremiah (5 times), Hosea (once), Jonah (once) and Habakkuk (4 times). Isa. 44.17 is an exception in other respects too, and convincingly proves the rule.[21]

Excluding the word <u>mošiaʿ</u>, since it may be either a noun or the participial form of the verb, no less than twenty out of the thirty-eight occurrences of HOŠIAʿ are nominalizations (YEŠAʿ, YᵉŠUʿA, TᵉŠUʿA). This is in striking contrast to HIṢṢIL, which occurs only in verbal forms, and this leads one to wonder whether the relative frequency of the two terms is partly a morphological matter. For instance, HIṢṢIL is less likely to occur in the construct-absolute relation than HOŠIAʿ, just because the corresponding nominal forms required by this construction (e.g. <u>kobaʿ</u> YᵉŠUʿA) are not available for HIṢṢIL. <u>haṣṣala</u> occurs only once in the OT (Esth. 4.14), and it may be plausibly suggested that YEŠAʿ, YᵉŠUʿA, etc. on occasion serve as nominalizations for HIṢṢIL as well as for HOŠIAʿ. In this respect we may distinguish HIṢṢIL from ʿAZAR and PILLEṬ as well, since they too occur as nominalizations. As distinct from HOŠIAʿ, ʿAZAR and PILLEṬ, the frequency of HIṢṢIL seems to be affected by the fact that it can only occur in contexts where nominalization is not required.

There is, however, another grammatical point of more direct relevance for a semantic description of these terms. As we have seen, HOŠIAʿ appears to be more likely to occur in collocation with metaphors like <u>markᵉbot</u> 'chariots', <u>magen</u> 'shield', <u>qeren</u>

'horn' and ŠA'AB mayim mimma'ayan 'draw water from a well', than HIṢṢIL. This has semantic implications: one might say, using Firth's language, that 'one of the meanings' of HOŠIA' is its collocability with magen 'shield'.[22] The collocational patterns available for HOŠIA', which has three nominalizations, and also for 'AZAR and PILLEṬ, are elaborate and rich in contrast to HIṢṢIL. In other words the associative field of HOŠIA' is, for purely grammatical reasons, much wider than that of HIṢṢIL.

2. The next feature to be examined is *transitivity*, and some preliminary remarks are needed. Like other linguistic phenomena, transitivity is not to be considered a permanent feature of any particular lexical item: it too is context-bound. A verb may be used transitively or intransitively, as for example English 'stand'; but this is not the same as saying that a particular verb is transitive or intransitive (sc. in every context).[23] Secondly, there is an important point about transitivity which was largely overlooked in the older text-books: some verbs are more transitive than others. It is possible to speak of degrees of transitivity. For example, 'build' is more transitive than 'die', but less transitive than 'bring'. The proof of this is a matter of probabilities: sentences like 'The house is building' (intrans.) are less frequent than 'They are building the house' (trans.) The words 'die' and 'bring', on the other hand, represent virtually total intransitivity and transitivity respectively.[24] As we shall see in a moment, HOŠIA' seems to be less transitive than the other members of its lexical group; but since this is based on probabilities, the size of the sample must be borne in mind.

Only HOŠIA' (9 times), 'AZAR (once) and PARAQ (once) occur without an object, but of these eleven cases only three can be taken as evidence for intransitive usage (see Table 3). Gen. 49.18 illustrates the reason for this: lišu'atka is a nominalization due to its combination with qiwwiti. As we saw, the question of exactly what the underlying structure is cannot easily be answered. Has an object been deleted? The same is true of HOŠIA' in I Sam. 2.1, Isa. 12.3, Jonah 2.10, Hab. 3.8, and of 'AZAR in Deut. 33.7. In all these cases the absence of an object may be due to the nominalization rules.[25] There are also two instances of the construction 'en + participle, in which the verbs concerned, HOŠIA' (II Sam. 22.42) and PARAQ (Lam.

5.8), do not have an object. Again this cannot be taken as evidence for an intransitive usage, since in both cases the participles may be nouns ('but there was no saviour'), and as such might again involve the deletion of the object.

TABLE THREE

Incidence of intransitivity in HOŠIA', HIṢṢIL, *etc.*

	Surface Structure	Deep Structure	Maximum
HOŠIA'	Gen. 49.18 I Sam. 2.1 II Sam. 22.42 Isa. 12.3 Jonah 2.10 Hab. 3.8	Jer. 14.9 Hab. 1.2 II Chron. 20.9	9 (25%)
HIṢṢIL			0
'AZAR	Deut. 33.7		1 (14%)
PILLEṬ			0
MILLEṬ			0
ḤILLEṢ			0
PASA			0
PARAQ	Lam. 5.8		1 (14%)

The maximum includes cases of surface intransitivity which may be due to the deletion of the object according to nominalization rules (see pp. 64,69).

HOŠIA', however does occur three times in a simple verbal construction without an object: Jer. 14.9, Hab. 1.2 and II Chron. 20.9. It is the only verb that occurs in this way, and this might suggest that in the doubtful cases quoted above HOŠIA', in contrast to the others, is intransitive too. The greater intransitivity, then, of HOŠIA', is a distinctive feature of this verb.[26]
3. Another characteristic of these items is their collocation, in many contexts, with the preposition <u>min</u> 'from'.[27] In this respect HIṢṢIL is clearly distinguished from the others: for while <u>min</u> occurs only 4 times with HOŠIA' (out of 38 times), and once with 'AZAR and PILLEṬ (out of 7 times), it occurs almost every time with HIṢṢIL. The only two cases where <u>min</u> does not occur with HIṢṢIL can be very satisfactorily explained as the result of interference from HOŠIA': in the first

instance (Judg. 10.15) it occurs immediately after, and in close relation with two occurrences of HOŠIAʿ (without min). When the same utterance occurs in another context (I Sam. 12.10) in which HOŠIAʿ does not occur, HIṢṢIL is followed immediately by min (miyyad ʾoyᵉbenu 'from the hand of our enemies'). The other case (Isa. 44.17) is a cultic cry addressed by an idolatrous craftsman to his wooden image. Here the simple substitution of haṣṣileni for hošiʿeni is probably to avoid giving HOŠIAʿ a subject other than YHWH, and gives an adequate explanation for the exceptional occurrence of HIṢṢIL without min.

HOŠIAʿ on the other hand occurs most frequently (34 out of 38 times) without min, and this provides an important semantic distinction between the two items HOŠIAʿ and HIṢṢIL. We might speak of a semantic component or an *element of separation.*[28] While all the items in this lexical group contain an element of separation, this applies above all to HIṢṢIL. HOŠIAʿ is distinguished by the absence of this element in most of the occurrences. The size of the register makes conclusions about the other terms in the group less reliable.

These conclusions are confirmed by another piece of evidence. The terms which contract relations with HOŠIAʿ, HIṢṢIL, etc., in poetic structure, can be divided into two groups: (1) spatial, in which the element of separation is prominent; and (2) non-spatial, in which other elements, emotional, psychological, social, etc. are detectable.[29] Straightaway the distinction already detected between HOŠIAʿ and HIṢṢIL is further clarified. Poetic structure brings the following purely spatial terms into relations with HIṢṢIL: HOṢIʾ 'to bring out', ROMEM 'to lift up', MAŠA 'to draw out', LAQAḤ 'to take', QIBBEṢ 'to gather together'. There is no instance of a non-spatial term entering into a relation with HIṢṢIL: and in every case the occurrence of min confirms the element of separation in the word.

HOŠIAʿ, on the other hand, is related by poetic structure to eleven items, only two of which are spatial, namely, HIŠPIL 'to bring down' and QIBBEṢ 'to gather together'. The other parallels present an entirely different picture: simple relations include ʿANA 'to answer', ŠAMAʿ 'to hear', RAPAʾ 'to heal', NIDHAM 'frightened', ZᵉROAʿ 'arm', ḤESED 'love'. Complex relations are contracted between HOŠIAʿ and HAṬAʾ 'to sin',

QARA' 'to call', QIWWA 'to hope' and ŚAMEAḤ 'to rejoice'.[30] Among these only one is followed by min. There is thus an element in common to all the terms related to HIṢṢIL and this element is almost entirely lacking from those related to HOŠIA'. This distinction convincingly parallels the evidence of the incidence of the preposition min 'from'.

On the slender evidence afforded by the register, it would appear that ḤILLEṢ is best grouped with HIṢṢIL at this stage, since it is related to HOṢI' 'to take out' and HIRḤIB 'to give room', both spatial terms. 'AZAR, with its parallels BEREK 'to bless' and GA'A 'to triumph', on the one hand, and HEBI' 'el 'ammo 'to bring back to his people', on the other, hardly exhibits any distinctive feature.

2. *Meaning-Relations*

> The meaning of a given linguistic unit is defined to be the set of (paradigmatic) relations that the unit contracts with other units of the language in the context or contexts in which it occurs.[31]

This important definition has been chosen as the starting-point for the main part of the present chapter. Now the meaning of HOŠIA', HIṢṢIL, etc. is well known already to anyone with a knowledge of Hebrew; but the precise definition of the meaning of these terms is far less readily available. The method implied in the above definition is based on certain relations contracted by the terms with each other and with other terms in the same language. The term 'paradigmatic' in the definition excludes 'syntagmatic' relations (i.e. those between a term and the other items in its context), and confines the analysis to relations between the term in question (e.g. hoši'eni) and all the other terms that can also occur in the same context (e.g. haṣṣileni, t^{e}śagg^{e}beni, r^{e}pa'eni). By analysing the linguistic contexts in terms of their underlying structure, we were able to identify paradigmatic relations involving HOŠIA', HIṢṢIL, etc. with more precision than was evident in their surface structures; but this does not affect the nature of the relations.

The phrase 'of the language' in the definition immediately precludes the meaning-relation most commonly used in dictionaries and commentaries, namely that between HOŠIA' and

TABLE FOUR

The Element of Separation

	Preposition min "from	Poetic parallels (1) Spatial		Poetic parallels (2) Non-spatial	
HOŠIA'	II Sam. 22.3	HIŠPIL	II Sam. 22.28	QARA'	II Sam. 22.4
	22.4	QIBBEṢ	I Chron. 16.35	'ANA	22.36
	II Kings 19.19				22.42
	Isa. 37.20			ḤESED	22.51
				Z^{e}ROA'	Isa. 33.2
				ḤAṬA	64.4
				QIWWA	Jer. 14.8
				NIDHAM	14.9
				RAPA'	17.14
				ŠAMA'	Hab. 1.2
				ŚAMEAḤ	II Chron. 6.41
HIṢṢIL	Gen. 32.12	LAQAḤ	II Sam. 22.17f		
	I Sam. 12.10	MAŠA	22.17f		
	II Sam. 22.18	HOṢI'	22.49		
	22.49	ROMEM	22.49		
	I Chron. 16.35	QIBBEṢ	I Chron. 16.35		
'AZAR	Deut. 33.7	HEBI'	Deut. 33.7	BEREK	Gen. 49.25
				GA'A	Deut. 33.29
PILLEṬ	II Sam. 22.44			ŠAMAR	II Sam. 22.44
MILLEṬ					
ḤILLEṢ		HOṢI'	II Sam. 22.20		
		HIRḤIB	22.20		
PAṢA					
PARAQ	Lam. 5.8				

1. 'Poetic parallels' include all terms related by the poetic structure to the term in question. See pp. 75ff.
2. Complex relations are underlined. See pp. 74f.

'to save', or between HIṢṢIL and 'to deliver' or between ʿAZAR and 'to help'. These important meaning-relations, on which the work of translation depends, are inadequate for precise description for several reasons: the cultural overlap between Hebrew and English, in particular that between OT Hebrew and modern standard English, is too narrow to ensure any consistent one-to-one relation between items in one language and items in the other.[32] What is more, relations between terms within Hebrew are apt to be obscured in translation: e.g. that between HOŠIAʿ 'to save' and TᵉŠUʿA 'victory'. One might add that if translation into English were an adequate method of defining the meaning of OT Hebrew, the task would have been satisfactorily completed already, and the present study rendered superfluous.

Another important relation that is commonly employed to define the meaning of an item is *synonymy* ('hošiaʿ means the same as hiṣṣil'). Clearly this is not sufficiently precise for our purpose, since what we require are distinctions between such closely related words. It is only one among several meaning-relations. Widely accepted statements like 'There are no real synonyms in a natural language',[33] and confusion with 'referential identity', must not be allowed to obscure the importance of synonymy. Like all meaning-relations synonymy must be bound to context and this is the basis of our present analysis.

A context where meaning-relations are contracted in a peculiar way in OT Hebrew, is the *structure of Hebrew poetry*. This represents a third, well-tried approach to the problem of defining the meaning of OT Hebrew. Both BDB and KB quote poetic parallels as aids to defining the meaning of Hebrew words. It depends on the fact that meaning-relations are contracted between lexical items in adjacent stichs or hemistichs. The term *parallelismus membrorum* is applied to this feature and it accounts for the majority of factors operating in Hebrew poetry.[34] A number of preliminary observations are necessary here.

In the first place a distinction must be made between *simple* and *complex* relations. In some cases the subjects of the terms in question are identical: for example, in I Chron. 16.35 the subject is YHWH throughout and the relation between the three terms HOŠIAʿ, QIBBEṢ and HIṢṢIL is thus a simple one. But let us look at Jer. 14.8:

A. miqwe yiśra'el
B. moši'o b^{e}'et ṣara
'hope of Israel,
their mošia' in time of trouble.'

Here the relation is between miqwe and moši'o, but the subject of the first is Israel (yiśra'el QIWWA b^{a} YHWH), of the second YHWH (YHWH HOŠIAʿ 'et-yiśra'el). The relation between HOŠIAʿ and QIWWA in this verse is a complex one. Similarly in Isa. 64.4 there is a complex relation between ḤAṬA' and HOŠIAʿ, since the subjects are different, ʿ^{a}naḥnu for the former and YHWH for the latter.

A second problem is that, while in the structure of Hebrew poetry the existence of meaning-relations is never in doubt, the precise nature of these relations is not dependent on the structure itself. If, for example, synonymy were the only meaning-relation contracted in poetic structure, semantic description would be considerably simpler. There are however a number of different types of *parallelismus membrorum* which can be detected only when the meaning of the terms involved has already been fairly closely defined.[35] Traditional terminology includes alongside 'synonymous parallelism', 'antithetic', 'synthetic', 'emblematic', 'stairlike' and 'introverted parallelism' as well. It is clear from this that the structure of Hebrew poetry, while indicating that a meaning-relation exists between two or more terms, does not provide a built-in definition of what relation it is, and cannot therefore be taken as a starting-point for semantic description. It may be possible on occasion, as we have seen, to detect a common semantic element in many of the items associated in poetic structure with a given term. But apart from this, poetic parallels are of secondary importance for semantic description, as confirmation, not independent definition.

Another point about poetic structure in OT Hebrew concerns the distinction, already referred to, between synonymy and referential identity. Let us take an example of 'synonymous parallelism' along with an example of the modern English literary device known as 'elegant variation':

A. *The Lord* thundered from heaven,
and *the Most High* uttered his voice (II Sam. 22.14).

B. The main philosophical influence was that of *Immanuel Kant. The Koenigsberg master* cannot himself be described as a Romantic, but was not unmoved by Rousseau.[36]

'The Lord' and 'the Most High' refer to the same reality, just as 'Immanuel Kant' and 'the Koenigsberg master' do; but this does not imply that they are synonymous. It is referential identity here, rather than synonymy, that is the basis on which the structure of the two passages depends. The literary critical term, 'synonymous parallelism', in other words does not mean that a relation of synonymy necessarily holds between every or any pair of terms in the two parallel members.[37]

Another important meaning-relation, frequently occurring in so-called synonymous parallelism, is *hyponymy*.[38] The following is quoted as a case of synonymous parallelism:

He has prepared his deadly weapons,
making his arrows fiery shafts (Ps. 7.13).

The relation between 'weapons' and 'arrows' however, is hyponymy, not synonymy; 'arrow' is a hyponym of 'weapon'. RAPA' 'to heal' is a hyponym of HOŠIA', not a synonym, in a verse like Jer. 17.14:

r^{e}pa 'eni YHWH w^{e} 'erape
hoši'eni w^{e} 'iwwaše'a.
Heal me, O Lord, and I shall be healed;
Save me, and I shall be saved.

That is to say, X RAPA' Y implies X HOŠIA' Y, but not conversely, since HOŠIA' may denote, not only physical healing, but also forgiveness and material help. The relation between HOŠIA' and many of the terms in its associative field can be defined as hyponymy. In poetic structure, however, the problem is more complex. The example just quoted involves not only referential identity, but also a type of semantic interference, whereby RAPA' takes on, in this context, a metaphorical meaning definable, after all, in terms of a synonymous relationship to HOŠIAʿ. In other words, poetic structure sometimes blurs the distinction between hyponymy and synonymy, and hinders rather than helps definition.

Reference is the relation that holds between a lexical item and an extra-lingual feature (referent):[39] for example, in Judg. 15.18, HOŠIAʿ is applied by the speaker (Samson) to a recent event in his experience, namely his victory over the Philistines, and the relation of reference is established by the demonstrative zoʾt 'this'. Ezra 9.13 is another example in which PILLET is directly applied to a known extra-lingual feature, namely, the return from exile. The problem of exactly what situation an utterance refers to has been dealt with at some length in an earlier chapter. In Jonah 2, II Sam. 22 and some of the Psalms, many of the lexical items can be partially defined in terms of their referents in particular situations, specified in the context of the utterances. A second problem arises from the first: often the speaker, beginning from his immediate situation (e.g. 'the day when the Lord delivered him from the hand of all his enemies and from the hand of Saul', II Sam. 22.1), meditates on the wider aspects of his experience. This generalizing process is an important element in doxological language, and has resulted in the almost unlimited applicability of religious texts like the Psalms. II Sam. 22 is a good example: in the first place vv.26-31 are a meditation on God's protection of those in need, which is clearly intended to be of wider application than the incidents referred to in the introductory sentence. But then the introductory sentence itself seems to suggest that the compiler was aware of the general applicability of this song: the incident in the Song is not just David's escape from Saul, but also his escape 'from all his enemies'. Thus meḥamas tošiaʿ, for instance (v.3), is applied to more than one incident in David's life. Finally this utterance is taken right out of its context in the narrative of II Samuel, and included in the Book of Psalms, which in itself suggests that a word like HOŠIAʿ is applied to an extra-lingual feature both in the immediate situation as described in the text, and in the wider experience not only of David but also of other members of the religious community to which he belonged. We can thus distinguish between *direct* reference, in which a unit is applied specifically by a speaker to one identifiable extra-lingual feature, and *indirect* reference, in which a unit is applied more generally. But it must be remembered that in cases of indirect reference, the immediate situation (or features in the immediate situation) may also be included in the application. The immediate situation, in other words, may be considered as an example of the general statement, and as such may provide important points of reference.

Examples of *consequence* and *implication* will illustrate their use, and the terminology associated with them. In II Sam. 22.50 the particle ʿal-ken 'therefore' brings HIṢṢIL into a (complex) relation of consequence with HODA 'give thanks':

me'iš ḥᵃmasim taṣṣileni
ʿal ken 'odka YHWH
. . . thou didst deliver me from men of violence.
For this I will extol thee, O Lord.

HODA is the consequent in this relationship, and HIṢṢIL the antecedent. An example of implication occurs in Isa. 44.17, where the particle ki 'for' brings 'el 'god' into a (simple) relation of implication with HIṢṢIL: haṣṣileni ki 'eli 'atta. Both HIṢṢIL and 'el are predicates of YHWH related to one another by the particle ki. There is no antecedent or consequent here, either in a temporal or a logical sense, and the prayer depends on the relation. In Ezra 9.15 the relation is the same, but the order reversed: ṣaddiq 'atta ki niš'arnu pᵉleṭa. ṣaddiq and PILLEṬ are brought into a relation of implication by the particle ki. Both are again predicates of YHWH, they are not synonyms, and in this case PILLEṬ comes second.

Collocation has been described as the 'basic formal pattern into which lexical items enter', and Firth's oft-quoted statement that 'one of the meanings of "dark" is its collocability with "night" ' has been applied in some subsequent theory as though it were the only adequate meaning-relation.[40] Collocation is, of course, a syntagmatic relation, and therefore by definition excluded from the present analysis. In any case since it is entirely a matter of probabilities (e.g. 'We are more likely to find HOŠIAʿ in the same utterance as the name YHWH, than šinnayim "teeth" and 'apa "to cook"), its adequacy as a semantic principle will be minimal in a sample of the size of the one we are working with.

There is however one type of collocation in OT Hebrew

which, while it is analysable as a syntagmatic relation in the surface structure of the sentence, may be rewritten as a paradigmatic one in its underlying structure. I refer to those construct-absolute relations to which the grammarians apply the term *genetivus epexegeticus* or *appositionis*. In expressions like ṣur yᵉšuʿati or qeren yᵉšuʿa, the paradigmatic relation between HOŠIAʿ and ṣur or qeren depends, like all metaphors, on a natural semantic connection or similarity between the two terms. But this connection is a loose one and one that scarcely assists definition. Indeed, when we have noted that HOŠIAʿ enters more frequently into this kind of relation and has consequently a richer associative field than the other members of its group we have virtually exhausted the information provided by collocation as a meaning-relation.

1. *Reference.* In the basic sentence A + HOŠIAʿ + ʾet – B + min + C + bᵉ – D, A, B, C and D all give the verb HOŠIAʿ a specific context of situation, in which lexical items are related to realities identifiable from the text (see Table 5). In two cases the verb itself is given a specific point of reference by the speaker: in Judg. 15.18 ʾet hattᵉšuʿa hazzoʾt is applied directly by the speaker to an identifiable event described in the preceding passage, namely, Samson's single-handed victory over the Philistines; and in Ezra 9.13 pᵉleṭa kazzoʾt is specifically applied to Israel's return from exile in the days of Ezra. Direct application by the speaker is rare, but in these two cases a clear relation of reference exists between HOŠIAʿ and the activity of YHWH in an identifiable situation, and between PILLEṬ and the activity of YHWH in another equally identifiable situation. The relation is more frequently established, however, for the subject, object and adjuncts of the verb, and this in turn puts the verb in a situational context in terms of which its meaning can be further defined.

(a) Only once does HOŠIAʿ occur with a *subject* other than YHWH and this is Hos. 14.4 (EVV 14.3), where the idea that Assyria should be the subject of the verb is repudiated by the speaker. The utterance is a pledge to turn again to the God of Israel:

TABLE FIVE

Reference to extra-lingual features

	A. Subject (other than YHWH)		B. Object (Other than speaker)		C. Object of Separation		D. Other Adjuncts	
HOŠIA‘	Assyria	Hos. 14.4	the king	II Sam. 22.51	injustice	II Sam. 22.3	invasion	Isa. 33.2
				Hab. 3.13	enemies	22.4	drought	Jer. 14.8
			priests	II Chron. 6.41	Sennacherib	II Kings 19.19	victory	Judg. 15.18
			the poor	II Sam. 22.28		Isa. 37.20	escape	II Sam. 22.51
			a righteous nation	Isa. 26.1f.			joy	Isa. 12.3
HIṢṢIL	wooden image	Isa. 44.17			Esau	Gen. 32.12	invasion	Judg. 10.15
					enemies	I Sam. 12.10		
						II Sam. 22.18		
						22.49		
						I Chron. 16.35		
‘AZAR	Meroz	Judg. 5.23			enemies	Deut. 33.7	victory	Judg. 5.23
								II Chron. 14.10
PILLEṬ					enemies	II Sam. 22.44	exile	Lam. 2.22
							return	Ezra 9.13
MILLEṬ					Sodom	Gen. 19.20	Zoar	Gen. 19.20
ḤILLEṢ								
PAṢA								
PARAQ					enemies	Lam. 5.8		

'aššur lo' yoši'enu 'al sus lo' nirkab
Assyria shall not save us, we will not ride upon horses.

HOŠIA' is never applied to the activity of anyone other than YHWH.

HIṢṢIL, on the other hand, is found in an idolater's prayer to his wooden image in Isa. 44.17. If, as we have just suggested, HOŠIA' is properly not applied to subjects other than the God of Israel, it would be natural to find examples of the intentional avoidance of the application of HOŠIA' to one other than YHWH. The implication of this would be that HIṢṢIL is of rather more general application than HOŠIA', and this is a conclusion confirmed by the rest of the OT. In language addressed to a deity, however, HIṢṢIL is never applied to the activity of a human being.

'AZAR is applied, even in language addressed to God, to human activity (Judg. 5.23). Here the subject is Meroz, one of Israel's allies. The context indicates that it would have been right for Meroz to be the subject of 'AZAR, and the fact that Meroz did not do so is held up as a reproach. This distinguishes the term from HOŠIA', a distinction forcibly confirmed by an examination of its occurrence outside the register as well.[41] The distinction may be described as a stylistic one, but it is nonetheless a real one and essential to a definition of the meaning of these words. In the register, HOŠIA' is reserved for the activity of the God of Israel, HIṢṢIL for divine agents in general, and 'AZAR is of more general application. The other verbs occur only with God as subject.

(b) In almost every instance the *object* of verbs in this group is the speaker or the speaker's community. The speakers themselves are Jacob, Samson, David, Hezekiah, Jeremiah, Jonah, Habakkuk and Hannah; the community is described variously as Israel, Judah, Joseph, Jeshurun and even, on one exceptional occasion, YHWH (sc. the army of YHWH) (Judg. 5.23). There are two exceptions: (1) HOŠIA' is applied to officials in Israel, namely, mašiaḥ 'the anointed one' (Hab. 3.13), melek 'king' (II Sam. 22.51) and kohanim 'priests' (II Chron. 6.41); (2) twice the object consists of a description rather than an identification: 'am 'ani 'the poor people' (as victims of injustice) (II Sam. 22.28) and goy ṣaddiq 'a righteous nation' (Isa. 26.1f.).

The verbs are without exception applied to the fate of the speaker, his own community or certain elements in it. Where any further definition of the object is given, it refers to the political or spiritual *élite* of the community.

(c) As has already been demonstrated, most of these words occur at least once with min- 'from'; it remains to examine the content of these prominent items. In every case the adjunct refers to the enemies or adversaries of the speaker(s). Where they are not specifically named, the reference is made clear in the introductory formula (e.g. II Sam. 22) or the immediate context (II Kings 19.19). In two cases the word ḥamas appears in collocation with HOŠIA' and HIṢṢIL, and here the reference is not merely a situation of danger at the hand of the enemy, but a situation of injustice.

Separation from enemies or other opponents, sometimes described as unjust, is a semantic element common to all the verbs in this group. There is no example of the converse, i.e. separation from friends or a situation of justice.

One final point in this connexion is that only HOŠIA' occurs with an impersonal min-adjunct, namely meḥamas (II Sam. 22.3). All the other adjuncts in the list are persons.

(d) There are a number of *modifiers* which have a specific point of reference in the situational context of the utterance. Extra-lingual features are deduced from the linguistic environment. When a temporal reference is made it is invariably to a crisis in the experience of the speaker(s). Other references are to the scale of the action described (its impressive nature is emphasized in two cases) or to the emotions which accompany it (e.g. rejoicing).

'AZAR is further distinguished from the others in its application to the activity of human warriors. The reference in II Chron. 14.10 is apparently to the situation of the weak confronted by a vast horde of foreign invaders. This aspect of the battle (580,000 Israelites under Asa versus one million Ethiopians and 300 chariots) is undoubtedly highlighted, but not to the same extent as, for example, the 'day of Midian' (Isa. 9.3; EVV 9.4), Samson's single-handed victory over the Philistines (Judg. 15), or Jerusalem's miraculous escape from Sennacherib in 701 BC (II Kings 19). The reference to the weak, however, agrees with the special mention of 'am 'ani in II Sam. 22.28.

2. *Opposition.* Opposition between lexical items, contracted either by the poetic structure of the utterance, or by some other syntactic structure in the sentence, is the simplest and most direct relation. It clearly excludes from the meaning of each member of the pair certain semantic elements. The other relations, synonymy, implication, consequence and the like, are often difficult to determine, although the existence of one or other of them is, in the context in question, indisputable. For example, while it is easy to identify the opposition between HOŠIA' and HIŠPIL in II Sam. 22.28, the exact nature of the relation between HOŠIA' and ŠAMA' 'to hear' in Hab. 1.2 is not so easy to define: that there is a meaning-relation there is established by the poetic structure; but is it a relation of synonymy (HOŠIA' means the same as ŠAMA' here) or implication (ŠAMA' implies HOŠIA') or consequence (HOŠIA' is a result of ŠAMA')? All these are structurally possible in the context; but it is hard to define which is semantically correct. For this reason, the method adopted here is to analyse the examples of opposition first, and then to examine the other meaning-relations together in the hope of differentiating them more precisely (see Table 6).

The clearest example of direct opposition is the one already referred to in II Sam. 22.28:

A. we'et 'am 'ani tošia'
B. wᵉ'eneka 'al ramim tašpil
Thou dost deliver a humble people,
But thy eyes are upon the haughty to bring them down.

Just as the respective objects of A and B 'the poor (i.e. innocent)'[42] and the 'arrogant', are opposed to one another, the verbs too can be sharply distinguished. An action described by the word HOŠIA' is not the same as one described by the word HIŠPIL. In Judg. 15.18 there is an opposition between HOŠIA' and MUT 'to die'. This is a complex relation (i.e. the subjects of the two verbs are different). The adversative use of wᵉ'atta 'but now' establishes the relation and the opposition is further developed in the word NAPAL 'to fall':

wᵉnapalti bᵉyad ha'ᵃrelim
Shall I now fall into the hands of the uncircumcised?

TABLE SIX

Meaning-relations

	Opposition		Consequence		Implication	
HOŠIAʿ	MUT	Judg. 15.18	ʾaš^{c}re	Deut. 33.29a	ʾEL	Deut. 33.29
	NAPAL	15.18	NIGGEN	Isa. 38.20	ʿANA	II Sam. 22.36
	HIŠPIL	II Sam. 22.28	BAṬAḤ	12.2a	SAMAʿ	Hab. 1.2
	QAṢAP	Isa. 64.4	HODA	I Chron. 16.35		II Chron. 20.19
	ŠEQER	Jer. 3.23			QIWWA	Jer. 14.8
	NIDHAM	14.9			RAPAʾ	17.14
HIṢṢIL			BAṬAḤ	I Sam. 12.10	ʾEL	Isa. 44.17
			HODA	II Sam. 22.19		
				I Chron. 16.35		
			ZIMMER	II Sam. 22.19		
ʿAZAR	NIKḤAŠ	Deut. 33.29b			ʾEL	Deut. 33.26
PILLEṬ					ṢADDIQ	Ezra 9.15
MILLEṬ			t^{c}ḥi napši	Gen. 19.20		
ḤILLEṢ					ḤAPEṢ	II Sam. 22.20
PAṢA						
PARAQ						

Complex relations are underlined.

The relation between HOŠIAʿ and nidham 'frightened' in Jer. 14.9 is one of opposition, as the negative particle loʾ indicates:

A. lamma tihye k^{e} ʾiš nidham
B. k^{e} gibbor loʾ yukal l^{e} hošiaʿ
Why shouldst thou be like a frightened man,
Like a mighty man who cannot save?

If X is frightened, he cannot be the subject of the verb HOŠIAʿ.

The interrogative form of Isa. 64.4b (EVV 64.5b) probably establishes a relation of opposition between HOŠIAʿ and QAṢAP 'to be angry':

A. hen ʾatta qaṣapta wanneḥṭaʾ
B. bahem ʿolam w^{e} niwwašeaʿ
Behold, thou wast angry, and we sinned,
In our sins we have been a long time, and shall we be saved?

If X is angry, how can he be the subject of HOŠIA'?

In Jer. 3.23 the opposition is between šeqer and HOŠIA' just as YHWH is opposed to haggᵉba'ot (i.e. heathen high-places).[43] A similar opposition exists between 'AZAR and KAḤAŠ 'to cringe' in Deut. 33.29.

HOŠIA', then, is opposed to the downfall of the arrogant, the death of Samson, the helplessness of a frightened warrior, the anger of an unsympathetic God and the deluding practices of heathen sanctuaries. These relations may be further grouped according to whether they concern the subject or the object of the verb: (1) the subject is not frightened, he is not angry, he is not a delusion; (2) the object is not thrown down, does not die, does not fall.

3. *Other meaning-relations.* In Deut. 33.29a a relation of consequence is established (by asyndeton) between HOŠIA' and 'asre:

A. 'ašᵉre yiśra'el
B. mi kamoka 'am noša' baYHWH
Happy are you, O Israel!
Who is like you, a people saved by the Lord?

The happiness of Israel is the consequence of the action described by HOŠIA'.

With this can be grouped a number of other passages in which a relation of consequence exists between the terms and various related expressions describing singing and praising God; e.g.

A. umoši'i me'oyᵉbai
umiqqamai tᵉromᵉmeni
me'iš ḥᵃmasim taṣṣileni
B. 'al ken 'odka YHWH baggoyim
ulᵉšimka 'ᵃzammer
. . . who brought me out from my enemies;
thou didst exalt me above my adversaries,
thou didst deliver me from men of violence.
For this I will extol thee, O Lord, among the nations,
and sing praises to thy name. (II Sam. 22.49f.)

The particle 'al ken 'therefore' identifies the relation of HOṢI',

ROMEM and HIṢṢIL to HODA 'to give thanks' and ZIMMER 'to sing'.[44] In this respect HOŠIA' and HIṢṢIL clearly agree.

A second recurring consequence is peace and security: e.g.

A. hinne 'el y^{e}šu'ati
B. 'ebṭaḥ w^{e}lo' 'epḥad
Behold, God is my salvation;
I will trust, and will not be afraid. (Isa. 12.2a)

Asyndeton again indicates the relation between HOŠIA' and 'ebṭaḥ w^{e}lo' 'epḥad. A similar relation occurs in I Sam. 12.10f. between HIṢṢIL and BAṬAḤ.

These relationships, however, although they admit of fairly precise definition, do not shed very much light on the content of the verbs under examination. In the first place they provide no distinctions as between one verb and another: all can be related to expressions of rejoicing and security. Secondly, statements of the form 'A + B + C result in X' actually tell us more about X than about A, B and C. Slightly more precise information about A, B and C can be obtained from the examination of another meaning-relation, namely implication.

A stylistic feature of the register is a motive-clause introduced by the particle ki: e.g.

haṣṣileni ki 'eli 'atta
Deliver me, for thou art my God! (Isa. 44.17)[45]

The efficacy of such a motive-clause depends on a relation between the verb in the imperative and a statement about YHWH, a relation best described as one of implication. 'If X is Y, then X HOŠIA'' can be expressed in the form 'Y implies HOŠIA''. This relation exists between HIṢṢIL and 'el 'god' in the passage just quoted, and between HOŠIA' and '^{e}lohim 'god' in II Kings 19.19, a fact which confirms the evidence discussed above under Reference. To these two examples can be added passages where the uniqueness of the relation is the point at issue:

A. 'en ka'el y^{e}šurun
B. rokeb šamayim b^e'ezreka
There is none like El, O Jeshurun,
who rides through the heavens to your help. (Deut. 33.26)

The relation of implication is between 'en ka'el yᵉšurun and 'AZAR. Deut. 33.29a provides another case of uniqueness in a relation between YHWH and HOŠIA', but here the uniqueness refers not to the subject YHWH but to the object Israel:

mi kamoka
'am noša' bᵃ YHWH
Who is like you,
  a people saved by the Lord?

Another case of implication in a motive-clause is Ezra 9.15, where PILLEṬ is related to ṣaddiq 'righteous'. The soteriological application of ṣedeq in OT Hebrew is well-known: it is interesting to have this confirmed here for ṣaddiq as well. Notice that it is not the justice of YHWH that is related to PILLEṬ: on the contrary the prayer of Ezra makes it plain that the people have not been dealt with according to strictly just principles. ṣaddiq, in other words, has a soteriological application here and little connexion with lawcourt justice.[46]

Another ki-clause brings the sentence YHWH tᵉhillati 'the Lord is my praise' into a relation of implication with HOŠIA' (Jer. 17.14).[47]

The following meaning-relations are contracted by the poetic structure:

A. yiš'u wᵉ'en mošia'
B. 'el YHWH wᵉlo' 'anam
They looked, but there was none to save;
  they cried to the Lord, but he did not answer them. (II Sam. 22.42)

A. 'ad 'ana YHWH šiwwa'ti wᵉlo' tišma'
B. 'eṣ'aq 'eleka ḥamas wᵉlo' tošia'
O Lord, how long shall I cry for help,
  and thou wilt not hear?
Or cry to thee 'Violence!'
  and thou wilt not save? (Hab. 1.2)[48]

It has already been suggested that the activity described by the word HOŠIA' is less physical than the other members of the group, and that the idea of physical separation is less prominent in HOŠIA' than in the others.[49] We now have the two passages just quoted, in which HOŠIA' is related to 'to answer' and 'to hear'. In II Sam. 22.36 there is another instance of this where 'ANA occurs in poetic parallelism with HOŠIA'. These are traditionally described as relations of synonymy (synonymous parallelism), but clearly this depends on a number of imponderables: is 'ANA used here simply in the sense of answering? Or has it the forensic sense of 'to testify in a court of law'? Whatever the conclusion reached on this question, there is little doubt that HOŠIA' is more closely related to these words, 'ANA, ŠAMA', etc. than any of the other words in the group.[50]

This conclusion is further justified when we consider another word related to HOŠIA' in more than one passage, but not to any of the others, namely QIWWA 'to hope'. Jer. 14.8 is an example:

> miqwe yiśra'el
> moši'o b^e 'et ṣara.
> O thou hope of Israel,
> its saviour in time of trouble.

The complex relationship between QIWWA (underlying miqwe) and HOŠIA' (underlying moši'o) is contracted by the poetic structure. Again, as in the case of the other parallels 'ANA 'to answer' and ŠAMA' 'to hear', moši'o seems to denote not so much actual physical intervention as readiness to intervene.[51] The same is true, finally, of RAPA' 'to heal' beside HOŠIA' in Jer. 17.14. Again the meaning-relation between the two words suggests that HOŠIA' denotes general health, physical and spiritual, rather than actual separation from a particular enemy or danger.

V

HISTORICAL DESCRIPTION

Enough has already been said on the subject of confusion as between the historical approach to linguistic description and the synchronic. The two levels of analysis must be kept distinct, and this has been done consistently throughout the present study. The prehistory of a word, however, may be a valuable source of information on its meaning in a particular context; and its subsequent historical development, too, may tell us something of its meaning or help us to understand some problematical feature of its usage in a particular context. Thus, while the meaning of HOŠIAʿ has been scrutinized as it is used in a particular situational context and in a particular linguistic environment, the analysis will not be complete without a survey of its usage outside this one context. The historical information on how a word was used in contexts far removed from the context under discussion, and the etymological information on how related terms are used in other languages, may or may not be relevant. Proto-Semitic background material may be more helpful in some cases than in others. The only way to find out is by a 'panchronic' approach.[1]

In his criticisms of the excesses of 'etymologizing', Barr to some extent underplayed the positive value of diachronic semantics. Very often the etymology of a word, however fascinating it may be, has little relevant information to offer on the meaning of a word as it is used in a particular context at a particular time by a particular writer, and 1961 was none too soon in the history of the semantics of biblical language for this point to be emphatically made.[2]

But there are several cases where the etymology of a word is not only an important part of semantic description but an indispensable one. In the first place, there is the recovery of a lost meaning. A word no longer in use in any living language, not attested in enough contexts to make synchronic description possible, and not occurring in a bilingual text cannot be described in any other way. Admittedly, in biblical scholarship words of this category are rare. But there are certainly terms, like miktam in the psalm-headings and d^{e}mešeq in Amos 3.12, which may be technical terms and whose precise meaning, judging by the wide divergence of opinion in the ancient versions, was already lost at least 2000 years ago.[3]

Secondly, there are cases where an author is known to have consciously exploited the etymology of a word for didactic or homiletical purposes. Examples from modern times are very common, and it is these that Barr so strongly attacked. But whether or not the 'wasiʿa-etymology' for HOŠIAʿ is correct, for example, and whether or not it has anything to do with how the word was used in ancient Israel, it can be consciously and quite successfully used in modern writing on OT language about salvation, since this type of 'etymologizing' has been fashionable and meaningful for at least two centuries. It may be compared to the equally illuminating semantic games played by ancient Jewish scholars. MKTM, for example, in Pss. 58.1 and 59.1, coming immediately after l^{e}dawid, could be translated in two halves as an epithet of David, *ταπεινοῦ τελείου* 'the humble (Hebrew mak) and perfect (Hebrew tam)'.[4] ṣalmawet 'the shadow of death' looks like another beautiful example of the same inventiveness.[5] Equipped with far more lexical data, modern successors to those ancient linguists are able to devise more elaborate conceits of precisely the same type. In both cases, knowing something about the interests and methods of the writer, we are able to work out how such and such a word is used. If it could be proved, for example, that a particular biblical author believed that Hebrew HOŠIAʿ and Arabic wasiʿa 'to be spacious' were related in some way, like 'Japheth' and Aramaic P^{e}TE 'to be wide' in Gen. 9.27, then the modern 'spaciousness-definitions' of HOŠIAʿ would apply to its usage in the context of his writings too. Where there is no evidence of this kind, however, Barr's criticisms are justified and must be heeded.

A third instance of a semantic exercise where historical information is indispensable is the study of one poorly documented stage in the history of a term. In a few contexts, for example, HOŠIA' apparently has a forensic sense: if 'an etymology could be found' to show that, at some stage in the term's history or pre-history, it denoted 'to defend (in a court of law)' or 'to testify' or the like, then the meaning of HOŠIA' in these few contexts in OT Hebrew would be illuminated.[6]

Some other interesting insights into the meaning of HOŠIA' in OT Hebrew emerge from a study of its prehistory in the second millennium BC; and the modern usage of the term is virtually unintelligible without reference to its use in the Bible.

In every case, however, the historical information must be ancillary to a synchronic study of the contexts where the terms under discussion occur. There is no other way of determining whether it is relevant or irrelevant, helpful or confusing, except by testing it against the contextual data. With these preliminary remarks on the role of historical semantics, we turn now to a historical description of HOŠIA', HIṢṢIL, etc.[7]

Recent theories concerning the historical background of the Hebrew language envisage a much larger language-group than used to be the case. The Hamito-Semitic family is to be divided into two groups, a more archaic southern group consisting of the Cushitic languages of Ethiopia and Somalia and the Chadic languages of Central West Africa, and a more progressive northern group consisting of ancient Egyptian and Coptic, the Berber languages of North Africa, and the Semitic languages, which stretch from Ethiopia in the south, through Arabia, Palestine and Syria to Mesopotamia in the east.[8] At all levels, phonological, grammatical and semantic, features of any of these languages are theoretically derivable from a common source. The triliteral root, for example, is a conspicuous feature common to all the languages in the northern group, and the same is true of the yqṯl forms of the verb. In practice, however, the influence of non-Hamito-Semitic languages, the vast chronological and geographical diversities involved, the role of chance in the survival of many of our sources, and the inadequacy of some of the scripts in which they were written, make this kind of derivation in many cases an impossibility, and in most cases an extremely difficult procedure. Hebrew lexicographers, however, nothing daunted, have for centuries worked on the hypothesis that any word in the dictionary of any one of the Semitic languages may be semantically related to any Hebrew word which has the same or a similar phonological structure. A great deal has been written in recent years sharply criticizing these 'inter-lexicon' activities.[9] The following seem to be the basic principles underlying recent discussions of the subject, including the present chapter.

1. *The phonological rules* must be observed unless there is very good reason for assuming an exceptional sound-change or correspondence. For example, where a Hebrew š̱ corresponds to Ugaritic and South Arabian ṯ, the correspondence between this sound and the Arabic s̱, which is required for the wasiʿa etymology, is exceptional.[10] There may of course be exceptions to any rule, but where the reasons for assuming an exception are, not that there is no other possibility, but that the etymological argument depending on it is particularly tempting, then we must think twice before accepting it.

2. *Chronology* is no less important. A word like ṣ^e daqa 'almsgiving', for example, is not likely to be helpful in defining words of the same root occurring, let us say, in Ugaritic, because this is a clearly traceable development from Biblical Hebrew to post-biblical Hebrew, and is not attested before that. One wonders how many Arabic words with a similar, but less well-attested history have been used to explain Biblical Hebrew words. Of course parallel developments may occur independently even in unrelated languages, and there is often the possibility of lexical borrowing; but neither of these two processes is the one in question in most of the philological discussions of this type. Classical Arabic, while extremely conservative in its phonology, is probably of all the Semitic languages the least conservative in its lexicon. This means that words which may easily be identified on phonological grounds as possible cognates of Hebrew terms, have nevertheless undergone hundreds of years of independent development which may have separated them semantically from their Hebrew cognates. It is here that the 'Ugaritophiles' are on stronger ground. There is good evidence, literary and historical, for a straight semantic development from Ugaritic of the fourteenth century BC to Biblical Hebrew from the twelfth century BC

onwards, and in this case the dangers are often less philological than text-critical.

3. *The priority of synchronic, contextual data* over the historical, comparative material has been emphasized from the beginning, and it applies here more than anywhere else. There are inevitably comparative philologists whose familiarity with several of the Semitic languages comes mainly from grammars and dictionaries, rather than texts. The present writer readily admits his own guilt in this respect. Yet few dictionaries provide nearly enough information to be adequate sources for comparative philology on their own. The *Chicago Assyrian Dictionary* is a conspicuous exception, and Ugaritic has not so far been quite so bedevilled by this problem, because the amount of literature extant is of manageable proportions, and contextual work has on the whole been an integral part of the area of comparative linguistics. But for Arabic, where the need is greatest for careful sifting of the material, no dictionary like the Assyrian one is available, and, until there is, philological arguments adducing Arabic cognates cannot achieve the same objectivity.

In the following historical descriptions the term 'root' is used as an abbreviation for 'root-morpheme' and denotes an identifiable group of consonants, not necessarily contiguous, which are common to a number of lexical items. Reconstructed forms, including roots, are marked with an asterisk, thus: *YŠ͑. '*YŠ͑-terms' and '*YT͑-terms' are shorthand expressions intended to avoid such cumbersome or misleading phrases as 'items containing the element *YŠ͑' and 'words derived from the root *YT͑'. Three stages in the history of a word or root are roughly distinguished: (1) the prehistory; (2) OT Hebrew, including occurrences of the terms outside the register; (3) later developments, e.g. Septuagint, Dead Sea Scrolls, New Testament, Talmud, Mediaeval and Modern Hebrew.

1. HOŠIA͑. The root *YT͑ is attested in a large number of proper names in two North West Semitic languages and most of the Epigraphic South Arabian languages. These correspond very closely to Hebrew names containing the root *YŠ͑ and provide convincing evidence for Proto-Semitic *YT͑ as the common factor.

Hebrew *YŠ' could go back to Proto-Hamito-Semitic *WS', which appears in Egyptian wśḫ 'to be wide' (causative śśḫ 'to widen, enlarge'), Berber usa' and Arabic wasi'a 'to be wide, spacious', but there is no contextual or semantic evidence for this reconstruction. A connexion between the two roots would involve two exceptional correspondences, namely, Egyptian s : Semitic ṯ, and North West Semitic ṯ : Arabic s.

The earliest occurrence of *YṮ' is probably in the Amorite personal name la-šu-il from Ur (*c.* 2048 BC). Analysable as la-yašu'-'il, the name contains an element corresponding to yašuḫ-/-ešuḫ in eight Amorite names from Mari (*c.* 1750-1696 BC). The same element appears again in the name yṯ'd, transcribed in cuneiform as ya-aš-ad-du, at Ugarit (fourteenth century BC). yṯ'il may be a shortened form of yṯ''il, and ya-šu-ia, the name of the leader of a revolt in southern Palestine referred to in an Amarna letter, may be another fourteenth-century example of a name containing *YṮ'.[13]

The earliest South Arabian example is Iti'amra (yiṯi'-amara), the name of a Sabaean king mentioned in Sargon's Annals.[14] Numerous other names in Safaitic, Thamudic, and Nabataean are also recorded with the element yṯ'. The causative stem, corresponding to Hebrew HOŠIA', is first attested in the elements hayṯa' or -hayṯi' in two Sabaean personal names.

The Ugaritic and South Arabian evidence clearly shows that the second consonant of the root was ṯ, written š in Akkadian cuneiform, and that the final consonant was ', written ḫ in Mari cuneiform, but not represented in post-vocalic position at Ur.[15]

Outside Biblical Hebrew, then, the term *YṮ' is relatively well-documented from about 2000 BC. It occurs only in personal names and like HOŠIA' in Biblical Hebrew is almost exclusively associated with the name of a god. The meaning of HOŠIA', YEŠA', etc. in Biblical Hebrew makes it probable that a verb *YAṮA'A in Ugaritic, South Arabian and elsewhere meant 'to help, save' or the like, but there is no evidence for the meaning of this common element.

An examination of the use of HOŠIA' throughout OT Hebrew confirms the evidence of the register, that the term is applied almost exclusively to divine intervention or the activities of divinely appointed agents such as kings and judges. A study of the word mošia' proved that it is the justice of the agent so described, in a situation of injustice, that distinguishes the word from semantically related terms.[16] It may be that we should translate moši'a' by a legal term like 'counsel for the defence' or 'advocate'.[17] hoši'eni has been defined as 'the usual legal formula' to be used by someone requiring legal assistance in a situation of injustice,[18] and we have already seen the prominence of legal terminology in the associative field of HOŠIA'.[19] We might add the frequency of proper names in ancient Israel and elsewhere, in which the name of a deity is combined with a legal term: e.g. Hebrew Yigael, Pedaiah; Ugaritic dnỉl, ṯpṭb'l; Assyrian Ashurdan, Nergalshaphat; Sabaean Yadan. A forensic origin for the *YṮ'-terms is possible, although as yet we have no evidence for this; a forensic usage for the *YŠ'-terms in OT Hebrew is probable.

The importance of the panchronic approach becomes obvious now: in a number of passages forensic features can be detected which would not have been evident without the historical factors. HOŠIA' collocates twice with ANA 'to testify' (II Sam. 22.36,42) and appears in a somewhat similar environment in Hab. 1.2. To these we might add the blessing of Dan in Gen. 49: whatever the historical connexion between v.18c and the rest of the passage, the possibility of a forensic link between HOŠIA' and the dan/yadin expressions would go some way towards explaining the choice of HOŠIA' in this passage.[20] It is the only occurrence of a *YŠ'-term in Genesis.

Three aspects of the later, post-biblical development of HOŠIA' concern us. First, its use in religious language continues in many set formulae based on or derived directly from the OT. It is common in the language of prayer, for example, and in the context of the Feast of Booths has been applied to a number of customs associated with the ritual: the lulab 'palm branch' or parts of it were termed hoša'na, and the last day of the feast is described as yom hoša'na or hoša'na rabba. The names of two settlements founded in Israel in modern times, yeša' and yiš'i, owe their origin to the orthodox religious interests of the settlers.

The forensic usage of moši'a' is attested in the rabbinic literature. In Modern Hebrew HOŠIA' is obsolete as a secular term for 'to help, save'. A tale is told in modern Israel, as an illustration of this, of the pedantic teacher who drowned because, when he shouted for help, he used the phrase hoši'eni 'save me!' and no one knew what he meant.

2. HIṢṢIL. *NṢL is attested in Arabic naṣala 'to fall out', V. 'to be free (from)'. Egyptian nḏ m- 'to save from the hand of'[21] suggests a common Hamito-Semitic origin, in which the element of separation, identified as a distinguishing feature of HIṢṢIL in Biblical Hebrew, was prominent. Syriac naṣṣel (Pa.) 'to free, save' is also attested.

By far the commonest occurrence of *NṢL in Biblical Hebrew is in the verb HIṢṢIL 'to deliver' with the passive NIṢṢAL. Once the Piel occurs in the same sense (Ezek. 14.14). The noun haṣṣala occurs once in the phrase rewaḥ w^ehaṣṣala 'relief and deliverance' from persecution (Esth. 4.14). Two other semantic facts can be noted. First, all the *NṢL- terms occur frequently in contexts of violent stripping off or spoiling (e.g. Ex. 3.22; Deut. 32.39; Isa. 5.29; Hos. 5.14; Amos 4.11; Pss. 7.3; 50.22; Job 5.4; Dan. 8.4,7), and a contrastive study of the use of mošia' and maṣṣil confirms this distinctive feature of the latter.[22] Second, the traces of a forensic usage were suggested by Daube in a brief comparison of the despoiling of the Egyptians and the taking away of a person's property in the Jacob-Laban story.[23] With this argument, which is hardly convincing on its own, should be compared evidence for a forensic usage of the Haphel (Aphel) in an Aramaic legal document from Elephantine, and the enigmatic pṣln, npṣl in the same papyri in the sense of 'to redeem' or 'compensate'.[24] Whatever the other divergences between HOŠIA' and HIṢṢIL, the possibility of interference or parallel development, particularly in this highly productive area of legal terminology, cannot be ruled out.

Finally, the use of HIṢṢIL with subjects other than the God of Israel confirms the suggestion, made with reference to the register, that this word is not 'disinfected' to the same extent as HOŠIA' in OT Hebrew.

In Mishnaic Hebrew HIṢṢIL is used in two contexts as well as conventional biblical formulae. First, it occurs in the sense of preventing a person from committing a crime (e.g. Sabb. 16.1; Sanh. 8.7); and second, in the sense of protecting a person from infringements of the ritual or levitical laws (e.g. Ohol. 5.3).

Several biblical idioms survive in Modern Hebrew usage, but in addition to these, NIṢṢEL 'to exploit', HITNAṢṢEL 'to apologize', NIṢṢOLET 'salvage', N^e ṢILUT 'efficiency' and the like make it clear that there is no religious peculiarity associated with the *NṢL-terms as there is with the *YŠʿ-terms. They have a much wider application in secular language. This feature, together with the prominence of an element of separation, decisively distinguishes HOŠIAʿ from HIṢṢIL throughout their historical development.

3. ʿAZAR. Amorite idru, Aramaic ʿ^a dar, Epigraphic South Arabian ʿḏr and Ugaritic ʿḏr 'to help, rescue'[25] suggests Proto-Semitic *ʿḎR. On the 'original meaning' two suggestions have been put forward: (1) 'to withold' (cf. Arabic ʿazara); (2) 'to excuse, exculpate' (cf. Arabic ʿaḏara). Of these the second involves no exceptional comparative phonology and gives good sense. But there seems no reason to suppose that the original meaning was not 'to help, rescue', and that the Arabic terms are examples of restriction of meaning. While being phonologically close to Proto-Semitic, Arabic may often have developed semantically further from Proto-Semitic than the other languages.[26]

In Ugaritic ʿḏr is followed by the preposition b 'from', and occurs in a number of proper names: e.g. yʿḏr, yʿḏrd, bʿlmʿḏr. In Ugaritic as well as the other Semitic languages where it is attested *ʿḎR-terms also occur in secular contexts.[27]

In OT Hebrew several *ʿḎR-terms occur as well as the more common *ʿZR-terms. This is undoubtedly due to lexical borrowing from Aramaic, a feature which we have already had occasion to mention in the HOŠIAʿ-field. Outside the register ʿAZAR presents a picture hardly distinguishable from that within it. The element of separation is indicated by the preposition min 'from' in only four passages: Deut. 33.7; Ps. 60.13 (EVV 60.12); 108.13 (EVV 108.12); Ezra 8.22. Among the subjects of ʿAZAR are false gods (e.g. Ezek. 30.8; Job 9.11), and the result of an action described by this verb is on occasion an evil one (e.g. I Kings 20.16; II Chron. 20.23). There are several proper names containing ʿZR-terms: Azarel, Azariah, Eliezer, Eleazar, Ezer, Ezra, and Jaazer.

In Talmudic Hebrew there is no trace of a technical or

restricted application, and in Modern Hebrew expressions like ʿezra rišona 'first aid' and ʿazarim ʾorqoliyyim 'audio-visual aids' further illustrate the wide secular semantic range of ʿZR-terms in contrast to HOŠIAʿ.

4. PILLEṬ, MILLEṬ. Evidence for Proto-Semitic *PLṬ 'to escape, survive' is to be found in Akkadian balaṭu 'to live, survive, escape' beside Aramaic pᵉlaṭ 'to escape' and a Piel (Pael) form in Ugaritic, Aramaic and Hebrew denoting 'to rescue'.[28] Personal names containing this last element include Ugaritic plṭ, yplṭ, Akkadian Ashuruballit, Phoenician plṭbʿl and Hebrew Pelatiah.

In OT Hebrew a biform MILLEṬ is attested which is semantically almost indistinguishable from PILLEṬ. The creation of a second term with similar meaning may be due to general factors contributing to the size of the HOŠIAʿ-field in Biblical Hebrew.[29] A complementarity as between the two terms is detectable however: PILLEṬ has no passive, NIMLAṬ (Niph.) 'to escape' occurs frequently: and while MILLEṬ has no nominalizations, PILLEṬ has three common ones: paliṭ, pᵉleṭa, miplaṭ. There are two distinctions in usage: (1) PILLEṬ 'to deliver' occurs mainly in the Psalms; MILLEṬ occurs only five times in the Psalms, of which three are the idiom MILLEṬ nepeš (Pss. 33.19; 89.49; EVV 89.48; 116.4); (2) the subject of PILLEṬ is always YHWH, while of the 27 occurrences of MILLEṬ YHWH is subject of only five (Pss. 41.2; EVV 41.1; 107.20; 116.4; Jer. 39.18 twice). In the register we noted that MILLEṬ does not occur in set-pieces, but only in conversational style, PILLEṬ occurs 7 times in the register.[30] The same appears to be true of Biblical Hebrew in general.

The two Hiphil forms, which each occur twice in Biblical Hebrew, may be due to interference, at the morphological level, from the more common terms HOŠIAʿ and HIṢṢIL: HIṢṢIL occurs in the same verse as HIPLIṬ in Isa. 5.29 and as HIMLIṬ in Isa. 31.5.

In Talmudic Hebrew three distinct terms appear, BALAṬ 'to stand forth', PALAṬ 'to vomit, escape'; MILLEṬ 'to rescue'. Of these the first and last need no comment, but the developments in PALAṬ, PILLEṬ appear at first sight unexpected. PILLEṬ (Piel) hardly occurs, being superseded by HIMLIṬ (Hiphil), although in Biblical Hebrew it was the commonest form; and PALAṬ 'to vomit', which is not attested at all in the OT, becomes common. The explanation of this development seems to be that PALAṬ 'to vomit' was actually a regular part of Classical Hebrew vocabulary, only by accident absent from the OT.[31] In Modern Hebrew the situation is the same: common secular terms for 'to escape' and 'to rescue' are NIMLAṬ and HIMLIṬ. PILLEṬ is derived from biblical language, and the other *PLṬ-terms are almost entirely confined to secular contexts (e.g. HIPLIṬ 'to eject, fire (a bullet)'.

It is only in the OT that all four occur together in the HOŠIA‘ field: MILLEṬ, PILLEṬ, HIMLIṬ, HIPLIṬ. In later Hebrew, at any one time, not more than two of these co-exist, another indication of the special nature of the OT and the peculiar size and structure of the HOŠIA‘-field.

5. ḤILLEṢ. Proto-Semitic *ḪLṢ appears to have both a transitive and an intransitive sense rather like English 'to withdraw'. Evidence for the former comes from Aramaic ḥᵉlaṣ 'to draw off, despoil', and for the latter Arabic ḫalaṣa 'to be purified, free'. Both senses occur in Hebrew ḤALAṢ (1) 'to take off (a sandal)' and (2) 'to withdraw'. The evidence for the sense of 'to save' outside the OT is slight: both Christian Arabic ḫallaṣa (II) 'to save', muḫalliṣ 'saviour' and ḫalaṣ 'salvation', and Phoenician ḥlṣb‘l could be due to borrowing from Hebrew.

Apart from two passages in OT Hebrew where the sense seems to be 'to tear out' (Lev. 14.40,43) and 'to despoil' (Ps. 7.5; EVV 7.4), ḤILLEṢ (Piel) occurs always in the sense 'to rescue, deliver', the subject is always YHWH and it occurs only in the Psalms (and Job 36.15). The element of separation, noted already in the prehistory of *ḤLṢ-terms, is indicated by the preposition min 'from' (Ps. 116.8; 140.2; Prov. 11.8) and spatial parallels (Ps. 18.20; EVV 18.19). There is one personal name in Biblical Hebrew, namely Helez, corresponding to Punic ḥlṣ and South Arabian ḫlṣ.

In later Hebrew two developments can be traced in the semantic history of the *ḤLṢ-terms: (1) in the forensic context of the levirate marriage, ḤALAṢ bayᵉbama to arrange the ḥ^a liṣa, act as judge'; and (2) in the context of war and national endeavour ḥaluṣ 'pioneer', ḥ^a liṣa 'battle-dress', etc. A religious settlement founded in Israel in 1950 has the name ḥeleṣ, which nicely combines the name of one of David's heroes (II Sam. 23.26) with ideals of ḥ^a luṣiyyut 'pioneering spirit'.

ḤILLEṢ (Piel) in Talmudic and Modern Hebrew has the sense of 'to extract', except in the idiom ḥilleṣ 'et-ha'^a ṣamot 'to take exercise'.

6. PARAQ. Proto-Semitic *PRQ can be reconstructed on the basis of Ugaritic, Hebrew, Aramaic, Arabic and Ethiopic. As to its meaning, there is evidence that a basic sense of 'to divide, separate' can be associated with the biradical stem p-r, a theory which undoubtedly fits the *PRQ-terms.[32] An element of separation is prominent in all the developments attested within the Semitic group: (1) restriction of meaning in a technical, forensic context, e.g. Aramaic p^e raq 'to redeem' (Targum Aramaic for Hebrew GA'AL), and Nabataean prq 'to buy back'; (2) a more general application in soteriological contexts, for instance, Ethiopic faraqa 'to set free', Syriac faruqa 'the Saviour'.

In Biblical Hebrew the normal usage of all *PRQ-terms (Qal, Piel, Hithpael) is in contexts of tearing away, snatching. The two occurrences in the HOŠIA'-field (Ps. 136.24; Lam. 5.8) are clearly the result of semantic borrowing from Aramaic, where the sense of tearing away or the like is not attested. There are no personal names containing *PRQ-terms in the OT.

In Talmudic and Modern Hebrew various secular developments take place: e.g. PARAQ 'to unload' (probably only by chance unattested in the OT), PEREQ 'to dismantle, discharge, liquidate (a company)', HITPAREQ 'to be factorized (mathematics), to relieve oneself'.

7. PAṢA. The solution to the problem of Aramaic paṣa 'to set free' beside Hebrew PAṢA 'to open' has been sought in Arabic faṣa 'to separate' as the basic meaning of a Proto-Semitic root *PṢY. We might add from our investigations into the HOŠIA'-field the evidence of PATAḤ 'to open' beside PITTEAḤ 'to save'.[33] That the two terms PAṢA 'to open' and PAṢA 'to save' both occur in Biblical Hebrew is best explained as a result of semantic borrowing, a recurring feature of this examination of

the HOŠIA‘-field.

PAṢA ‘to save’ occurs only in Ps. 144, where it occurs three times. The element of separation is indicated twice by collocation with HIṢṢIL min, and once by the preposition min. The psalm used to be given a late date, and Aramaisms were adduced as evidence for this; but its relationship to the Karatepe inscription and its royal characteristics have led scholars more recently to date it certainly before the exile.[34] This view would have interesting implications for a history of semantic borrowing from Aramaic in Biblical Hebrew.

In later Hebrew PAṢA ‘to open (the mouth)’ is frequently attested. PIṢṢA (Piel) ‘to compensate’ can be traced to a forensic usage in Talmudic Aramaic. PAṢA (Qal) ‘to save’ is superseded, like PILLEṬ, HIPLIṬ, ḤILLEṢ and PARAQ, by other terms, and again the peculiarly rich associative field of HOŠIA‘ in OT Hebrew is impoverished in the later history of the language.

VI

DEFINITION

The problem of how to tabulate the heterogeneous information on each of the lexical items discussed is not an easy one. A definition must make available for the translator and the exegete, as well as the Semitist or general linguist, such facts about each item as he will need, without introducing unnecessary terminology or burdening him with superfluous details. There is no reason in the case of Biblical Hebrew, for example, to duplicate the work of concordance-compilers. Existing lexica already list many of the occurrences of each word under certain semantic headings. But what is still to be done is to present the distinctive features of each item as described above, and this means constant reference to the semantic field in which it occurs. BDB and KB present no systematic examination of this feature of linguistic description: BDB mentions 'synonyms' or other poetic parallels in many entries, thereby drawing attention to similarities in meaning, but rarely notes the differences in meaning between them. If there is one matter on which all modern semantic theorists are agreed, it is the centrality of opposition in all descriptive analyses, and it is on this principle that all the following sets of definitions are based. Percentages are approximate, and, being based on a small sample, are mainly of methodological interest, although a survey of the terms as they are used outside the register confirms most of the conclusions.

1. *HOŠIA' is distinguished from HIṢṢIL as follows:*

(a) Frequency. HOŠIA' is five times more frequent than HIṢṢIL. There are indications that HOŠIA' is the proper word

for use in language addressed to the God of Israel; HIṢṢIL may on occasion be used to avoid an improper usage. HIṢṢIL is not frequent in the prophets; HOŠIA' is most frequent there.

(b) Nominalization. There are no nominalizations of HIṢṢIL in the register (only one in OT Hebrew); HOŠIA' has four which occur regularly. Of the recorded occurrences of HOŠIA' 50% are nominalizations, and this has the following results: (i) HOŠIA' occurs very frequently in metaphorical expressions like qeren y^{e}šu'ati 'the horn of my salvation' and ma'^{a}yane hay^{e}šu'a 'wells of salvation'. HIṢṢIL is never found in this type of construction, and its associative field is therefore poorer than that of HOŠIA'. (ii) HOŠIA' occurs with a qualifier like gadol 'great', and again the semantic range of HOŠIA' is wider and more colourful than that of HIṢṢIL.

(c) Transitivity. HOŠIA' is intransitive at least three times in the register (8%) and possibly as many as nine times (25%);[1] HIṢṢIL does not occur without an object. HOŠIA' is perhaps closer in meaning to an English intransitive verb like 'to intervene' in some contexts.

(d) Element of separation. HIṢṢIL is accompanied, apart from one exceptional case, by the preposition min 'from'; HOŠIA' occurs in this kind of collocation only four times in the register. It may be concluded that while HIṢṢIL regularly involves the separation of one object from another, HOŠIA' normally denotes an action not involving any idea of separation. The historical evidence for *NṢL-terms in other languages confirms this.

HIṢṢIL is associated in various types of meaning-relation with terms like HOṢI' 'to bring out', ROMEM 'to lift up' and MAŠA 'to draw out', which may all be described as spatial terms; HOŠIA' is commonly associated with non-spatial, medical or psychological terms like RAPA' 'to heal', 'ANA 'to answer', and ŠAMA' 'to hear'.

(e) Religious context. There is some evidence that HOŠIA' is one of a small group of 'disinfected' words (cf. BARA' 'to create'), properly used only in contexts where YHWH or his appointed leader is subject, its application in other contexts being consciously avoided and even explicitly condemned. HIṢṢIL appears to be used in one context to avoid such an improper usage; and a relation of implication which holds

between the name of a deity and both HOŠIA' and HIṢṢIL confirms this, since the deity involved in the first case is the God of Israel, in the second a wooden idol.

2. HOŠIA' *is distinguished from* 'AZAR *as follows:*

(a) Frequency. HOŠIA' is five times more frequent in language addressed to God than 'AZAR. 'AZAR never occurs in HITPALLEL-utterances and only once in a ŠIR-utterance; HOŠIA' is particularly frequent in these two styles. 'AZAR occurs mainly in BEREK- and QARA'- utterances where HOŠIA' is rare.

(b) Religious Context. HOŠIA' is applied properly only to the activity of the God of Israel; 'AZAR is the only member of the lexical group that occurs, even in language addressed to God, with a human subject.

3. HOŠIA' *has the following features in common with* 'AZAR *against* HIṢṢIL:

(a) Nominalization. More than 50% of the occurrences of 'AZAR in the register are nominalizations. Expressions like magen 'ezri 'the shield of my help' bring 'AZAR closer to HOŠIA' semantically than HIṢṢIL, and indicate the richer associative field against which 'AZAR too must be viewed.

(b) Element of separation. Unlike HIṢṢIL, 'AZAR is followed only once by the preposition min 'from'. The possibility of semantic interference is possible (cf. ŠAPAT, RIB), and brings 'AZAR and HOŠIA' into the same part of the field.

4. HIṢṢIL *is distinguished from* 'AZAR *as follows:*

(a) Frequency. Although both occur with the same frequency in the register, their stylistic distribution is different: HIṢṢIL does not occur in the two styles in which 'AZAR is most frequent. The one occurrence of 'AZAR in a style in which HIṢṢIL also occurs is exceptional.

(b) Nominalization. HIṢṢIL is distinguished both from 'AZAR and HOŠIA' in this respect: no nominalization occurs in the register and this may be said to impoverish the semantic range of HIṢṢIL in contrast to the other two terms.

(c) Element of separation. HIṢṢIL stands apart from both 'AZAR and HOŠIA' in this respect too: It almost exclusively

occurs with the preposition min 'from'.

5. MILLEṬ, PILLEṬ, ḤILLEṢ, PARAQ, PAṢA are much less frequent than the other terms. PAṢA does not occur at all in the register; MILLEṬ only in conversational style. Both PILLEṬ and PARAQ are followed by min 'from'. Other than this the evidence of our register is insufficient to base further semantic conclusions.

A second method of definition involves the systematic tabulation of the information, both synchronic and historical, which has been amassed in Chapters II to V above. Each entry begins with a list of all the lexical items which belong to the same semantic field as the word being defined, so that oppositions can be noted at every stage of the description. The semantic field is introduced by the transparent sign 'cf.' and within the field opposition is marked thus 'X̌'. Under HOŠIA', then, the reader is automatically referred to all the words most closely related to it semantically. This also implies that, in conjunction with a concordance, it is possible to trace a very large number of contexts relevant to a study of salvation in the OT, and not just those in which HOŠIA' occurs. Each item's frequency in OT Hebrew is listed immediately after the group of related terms.

All the available semantic material is then presented as follows: significant structural features (transitivity, nominalization, etc.) make up the first paragraph, contrasts and comparisons with other members of the group being indicated in each case. The second paragraph gives the usage of the word in OT Hebrew, and at this stage English equivalents are suggested. It should be noted that exceptional usages are not listed here so that the reader may obtain an idea of the normal usage of the word against which to measure each occurrence as he deals with it in the text. The English equivalents are intended to reflect structural features and semantic characteristics already listed in the article: thus 'to intervene' in the HOŠIA' entry takes up the point made earlier that the word is more intransitive than the other terms.

Finally, and the position is not without significance, the etymology is discussed. The reconstructed Proto-Semitic roo is followed by a reconstructed meaning, wherever possible, and this is followed by various lines of development attested throughout the Hamito-Semitic family. The practice adopted by the *Oxford Dictionary of English Etymology*, whereby the earliest attested occurrence of each item is dated as far as possible to the nearest century, has been followed, with the refinement demanded by the subject matter, that dates BC are indicated by Roman numerals in lower case (e.g. Ugaritic xiv.; Moabite ix.), while dates AD are indicated by capitals (e.g. Aramaic II.; Hebrew XX.). Sources for the information selected for each article might be listed in a final paragraph.[2]

The entry is thus intended to present a general definition of each item as it is most often used in OT Hebrew. Abnormal usages must be dealt with in the commentaries. These definitions are based in the first instance on details obtained from the register; but these have been implemented by a survey, albeit rather less detailed, of the rest of OT Hebrew. In fact it emerges from this comparison that the register provided a remarkably representative sample, and conclusions based on it are often confirmed by conclusions based on the wider study. Percentages are again approximations, and are only quoted when significant. Statistics are based on Mandelkern.

HOŠIA' Cf. HIṢṢIL ḤILLEṢ MILLEṬ 'AZAR PAṢA PARAQ PILLEṬ.
337 instances (183 Hiphil, 20 Niphal, 134 nominalizations).
Nominalizations (yeša', y^e šu'a, t^e šu'a, moša'ot): 43% cf. 'AZAR, PILLEṬ.
Transitivity: 89% X HIṢṢIL, ḤILLEṢ, etc.
Separation: 10% X HIṢṢIL, cf. 'AZAR, PILLEṬ.

1. Religious contexts (prophetic books, Psalms, 'set-piece' style): 95% X 'AZAR, MILLEṬ, ḤILLEṢ, 'to save', 'salvation'; 'to intervene'.

2. Forensic contexts (Deut., Josh., Judg., Sam., Kings; fig. Psalms, Isaiah): 5% (esp. mošia') cf. HIṢṢIL (GA'AL, ŠAPAṬ, etc.), 'to defend', 'defence'.

Proto-Semitic *YṮ' to help, save' (?):
1. yṯ' 'to save'(?): xx. Only in theophoric names, e.g. Amorite la-šu-il (la-yašu'-il), a-ḫi-ya-šu-uḫ; Ugaritic yṯ'd (ya-aš-ad-du);

Sabaean Iti' amra (yiti'-'amara); Nabataean yṯ'w.
2. hošia' 'to save': x. Religious context (OT Hebrew, Moabite; loanword in Samaritan).
3. *YŠ' 'to be spacious': XVIII. Folk etymology, cf. Arabic wasi'a, Egyptian wśḫ.

HIṢṢIL Cf. HOŠIA' ḤILLEṢ MILLEṬ 'AZAR PAṢA PARAQ PILLEṬ.
203 instances (186 Hiphil, 15 Niphal, 1 Hithpael, 1 nominalization).
Transitive X HOŠIA'.
Separation: 90% X HOŠIA', 'AZAR.

1. Religious contexts: 80% 'to deliver'.
2. Forensic contexts (?): rare cf. HOŠIA' 'to redeem'.

Proto-Hamito-Semitic *NṢL 'to remove, take away':
1. xxv. General use (e.g. Egyptian nḏ 'to save [from] '; Hebrew hiṣṣil 'to deliver'; Arabic tanaṣṣala 'to be free [from] ').
2. vi. Legal documents (Aramaic), 'to redeem'.

ḤILLEṢ Cf. HOŠIA' HIṢṢIL MILLEṬ 'AZAR PILLEṬ PAṢA PARAQ.
18 instances (14 Piel, 4 Niphal).
Transitive X HOŠIA'.
Separation: 45% X HIṢṢIL.

1. Religious contexts (Psalms, Job, Prov.): 75% cf. HIṢṢIL, 'AZAR, 'to deliver'.
2. General contexts (Lev., Num.): 'to strip, pull out (stones)'.

Proto-Semitic *ḪLṢ 'to withdraw':
1. ḥalaṣ (trans.) 'to take off': x. 'to strip for battle' (e.g. Hebrew, Aramaic).
2. ḥalaṣ (intrans.) 'to withdraw': viii. (e.g. Hebrew, Arabic).
3. ḥilleṣ 'to deliver': x. Religious contexts (Hebrew, loanword in Arabic, Phoenician).

MILLEṬ Cf. HOŠIA' HIṢṢIL ḤILLEṢ 'AZAR PILLEṬ PAṢA PARAQ.
89 instances (58 Niphal, 27 Piel, 2 Hiphil, 2 Hithpael).

Transitive X HOŠIA'.
Separation: 69% cf. HIṢṢIL.

1. General use *(passim):* 'to rescue, escape (Niphil)' X PILLEṬ.
2. MILLEṬ nepeš *(passim):* 'to save one's life'.

Proto-Semitic *PLṬ 'to live'. Cf. PILLEṬ.

ʿ**AZAR** Cf. HOŠIAʿ HIṢṢIL ḤILLEṢ MILLEṬ PILLEṬ PAṢA PARAQ. 137 instances (86 Qal, 4 Niphal, 1 Hiphil, 46 nominalizations).
Transitive X HOŠIAʿ.
Nominalization (ʿezer, ʿezra): 40% cf. HOŠIAʿ, PILLEṬ.
Separation: 1% cf. HOŠIAʿ, PILLEṬ.

General use *(passim):* 'to help'.

Proto-Semitic *ʿḎR 'to help':
1. ʿḏr 'to help, save (from)': xiv. (Ugaritic, hence Arabic ʿaḏara to exculpate');
2. ʿadar 'to help': xviii. (Amorite, Aramaic; loanword in OT Hebrew).
3. ʿazar 'to help': xii. (Hebrew, Phoenician).

PILLEṬ Cf. HOŠIAʿ HIṢṢIL ḤILLEṢ MILLEṬ ʿAZAR PAṢA PARAQ.
79 instances (24 Piel, 2 Hiphil, 53 nominalizations).
Transitivity: 96% cf. HOŠIAʿ.
Nominalization: 75% cf. HOŠIAʿ, ʿAZAR.
Separation: 12% cf. HOŠIAʿ.
1. Religious contexts (Psalms): 93% 'to save' cf. HOŠIAʿ.
2. General use (esp. paliṭ, pᵉleṭa): 'survivor', 'to escape', cf. MILLEṬ.

Proto-Semitic *PLṬ 'to live':
1. balaṭu 'to live, recover': xx. (Akkadian; hence II. balat in Aramaic, Hebrew).
2. palaṭ 'to survive': ix. (Aramaic, Hebrew, Phoenician).
3. pilleṭ 'to save': xiv. (Ugaritic, Hebrew, Aramaic).
4. milleṭ 'to rescue': x. (Hebrew).

PAṢA Cf. HOŠIA' HIṢṢIL ḤILLEṢ MILLEṬ 'AZAR PILLEṬ PARAQ.
3 Instances (Qal).
Transitive X HOŠIA'.
Separation: 100% cf. HIṢṢIL, PARAQ.

Religious contexts (Psalms): 'to set free' cf. HOŠIA'.

Proto-Semitic *PṢY 'to separate':
1. paṣa 'to open': x. (Hebrew).
2. p^e ṣe 'to set free': (Aramaic; loanword in OT Hebrew).
3. piṣṣa 'to compensate': II. (Aramaic, Hebrew).
4. faṣa 'to separate': ? (Arabic);

PARAQ Cf. HOŠIA' HIṢṢIL ḤILLEṢ MILLEṬ 'AZAR PILLEṬ PAṢA.
4 instances (Qal).
Transitive X HOŠIA'.
Separation: 100% cf. HIṢṢIL, PAṢA.

1. Religious contexts (Psalms, Lam.): 'to set free' (persons), cf. HOŠIA'.

2. General use (Gen., Psalms): 'to tear away' (things), cf. ḤILLEṢ.

Proto-Semitic *PRQ 'to separate':
1. paraq 'to split': x. (Hebrew, Aramaic; cf. Arabic faraqa).
2. p^e raq 'to set free': v. (Aramaic, Syriac, Ethiopic; loanword in OT Hebrew).

Thirdly, some semantic information, particularly data drawn from a closed literary corpus like the OT, is quantifiable and it should therefore be possible to represent it graphically. The last proposal for defining Hebrew terms for salvation is a very tentative one, and is merely intended to illustrate the kind of visual representation that might be useful.

The six commonest Hebrew terms for salvation are plotted in four sectors. Each sector contains percentages of the total number of occurrences of the terms in the OT (given in brackets after each term). According to the first sector, for example, approximately 95% of the 337 occurrences of HOŠIA' in OT Hebrew have as subject YHWH or an Israelite leader appointed by him; in contrast to MILLEṬ which occurs in similar contexts in less than 50% of its total occurrences. It may be that four sectors are not enough to give a useful picture of semantic distinctions in every part of the Hebrew lexicon; but in this case, where there are six closely related terms, some broad distinctions become clearly apparent in the diagrams. Statistics on the element of separation in the second sector are based on the occurence of min 'from' or collocation with spatial terms like HOṢI' 'to bring out'. Transitivity, which here applies only to verbal forms, provides an interesting distinction between HOŠIA' and the other five terms; and nominalization gives important information on the size and structure of each term's associative field. Percentages are again approximate and are based on statistics taken from Mandelkern.

HOŠIA' and PILLEṬ stand closest together in the diagram. With them must be grouped 'AZAR, which, although it is less restricted to religious contexts, has a very similar 'shape'. The other three terms form a separate group. Perhaps the most interesting opposition between the two groups is that between PILLEṬ in the first group and MILLEṬ in the second, terms which historically are closely related. Of the HOŠIA'-group only one term, 'AZAR, remains in common use in later Hebrew. This is the kind of semantic grouping that can be represented diagrammatically, and which does not become so immediately evident by other methods of definition.

(1) HOŠIA' (337 times)

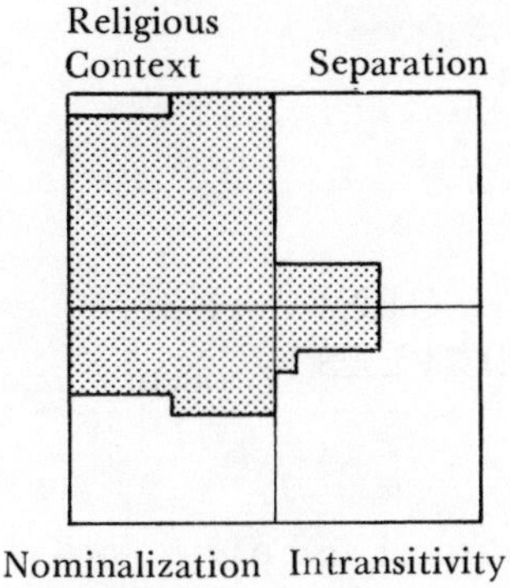

(2) HIṢṢIL (203 times)

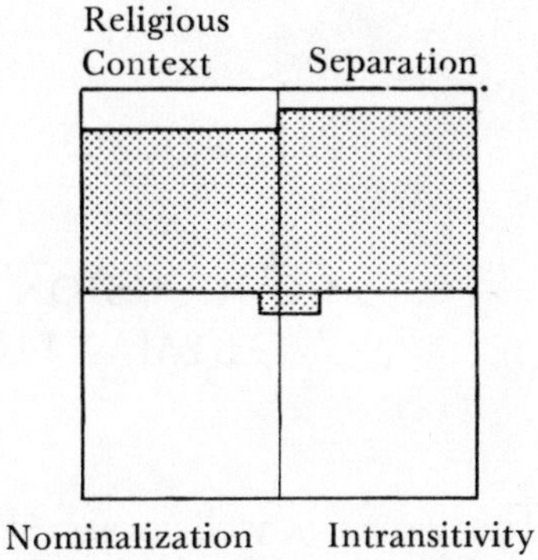

(3) ḤILLEṢ (18 times)

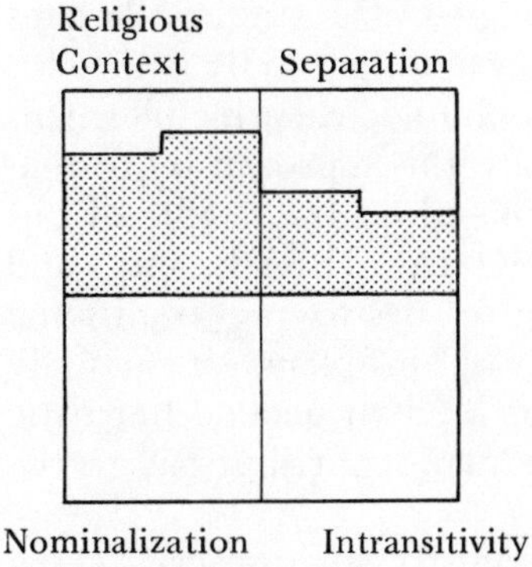

(4) MILLEṬ (89 times)

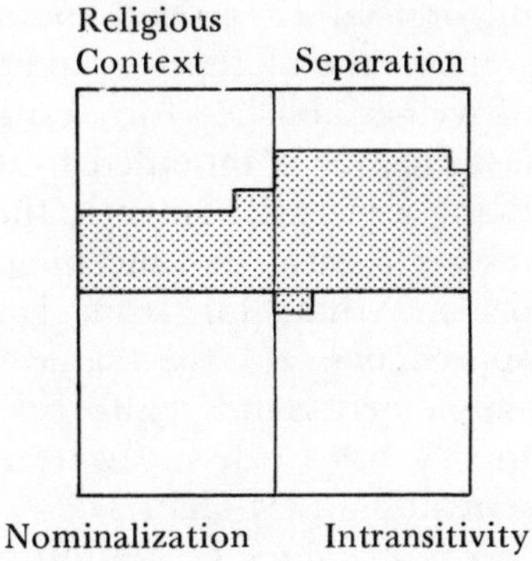

(5) 'AZAR (137 times)

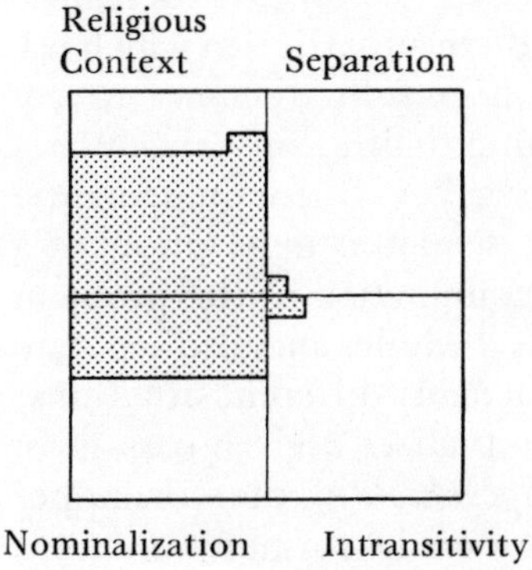

(6) PILLEṬ (79 times)

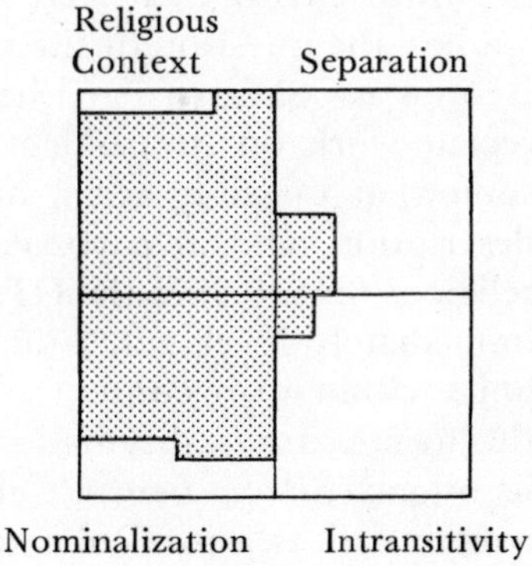

VII

CONCLUSION – SOME GENERAL SEMANTIC PRINCIPLES

The writer is well aware of the historical and psychological barriers that exist between biblical scholarship and linguistics today. He knows only too well that much of the terminology introduced above will sound foreign in OT studies. Perhaps some of the methods used appear at first sight to fly in the face of well-established form-critical or philological principles. This last chapter is intended to vindicate the approach by formulating a general semantic theory, based on the results of our research into the meaning of HOŠIA', HIṢṢIL, etc., and proving that, far from ignoring or destroying traditional approaches to the same kind of problem, it actually supplements and reinforces them. Modern general linguistic theory has made us aware of five main contributions to the semantics of OT Hebrew.

1. *An adequate definition of context must precede every semantic statement.* While the importance of immediate linguistic environment has been noted in previous semantic studies, the question of the situation or situations in which OT Hebrew is contextualized has not been fully discussed in any recent work on the subject. 'Contextualization', although a somewhat ungainly term, denotes a key factor in semantic description, and in particular the semantic description of a religious text such as the OT. An examination of this problem immediately reveals that the OT as a whole, and also separate units within it, are contextualized in many different situations: the form-critic traditionally contextualizes a given passage in its original *Sitz im Leben (Gattungsgeschichte);* the worshipper contextualizes a particular psalm or credal formulation in his

own experience at the present (actualization); the religious teacher contextualizes parts of the legal codes in the life of his community (authority); the preacher contextualizes prophetic passages in contemporary history (application). The first step in semantic description, then, must be to make clear which context of situation has been selected.

A consequence of this conclusion was to question the widespread assumption that the original contextualization is necessarily the most important. This presupposition can be traced back to the *cognicio historiae* which Luther saw as a necessity for biblical exegesis but which referred only to the original context of situation.[1] Is the 'original meaning' of HOŠIA' as reconstructed by eighteenth- and nineteenth-century comparative philologists more important than its meaning as attested in OT Hebrew? Our standard lexica suggest that it is. But it is an essential part of semantic theory that this selection of one contextualization out of many is seen to be an arbitrary one. The church traditionally describes the meaning of Isa. 7.14 with reference to Jesus Christ, and the present writer believes this description to be meaningful and true. But here the semanticist (lexicographer, exegete, or theologian) is stepping outside his terms of reference. He may do this for two reasons: either for convenience, since a complete analysis of the meaning of a word or a passage in every situation in which it is contextualized would take a lifetime, or because of a particular, personal interest in one or other of the situations. For instance the form-critic, thanks to a mass of archaeological evidence, would naturally be interested in the original situation in ancient Israel; the New Testament scholar would be interested in the early church and the contextualization of OT Hebrew in the experiences of a Christian community.

The isolation of this problem of contextualization led to a further question that must be dealt with before an adequate semantic description is possible, namely the nature of the OT. As a religious text, it has a number of characteristics of importance to semantic theory: the language is peculiarly fitted for contextualization in a wide, one might almost say, infinite number of situations; there are words of exclusively religious application, like BARA' 'to create' and to a lesser extent, HOŠIA' 'to save'; there is a tendency to minimize ambiguity, meaninglessness and irreverence in the text; the size of certain lexical groups, such as HOŠIA', HIṢṢIL, etc., is exceptionally large in comparison with the situation in later Hebrew; and finally the corpus is not a representative cross-section of the Hebrew language at any one time.[2] These contextual factors have numerous implications for the linguist, and must be stated at the outset.

2. *Semantic statements must be primarily synchronic.* By this is meant, not that diachronic (historical) statements are invalid, but that they are inevitably based on synchronic statements, and must therefore only be made after adequate synchronic description has been completed. The semanticist freezes, as it were, the historical development of a word or a passage at a certain point and analyses it there first. This may involve the introduction of historical information: for example, to give an adequate description of HOŠIA' in Modern Hebrew, one would have to refer to its meaning in the OT. But historical, i.e. etymological statements can never precede synchronic description: they are always ancillary to the semantic description of a word in its context.

This implies that, for adequacy as well as convenience, a single point in the development of the language (or the interpretation of the language) is to be selected as a starting-point. The above description of HOŠIA', HIṢṢIL, etc. was limited to masoretic tradition as printed in Kittel's *Biblia Hebraica.* Within it a particular register was selected rather than a particular literary form or chronological stratum, first because this seemed more in accordance with the nature of the text, and second because the register in question, language addressed to a deity, was an interesting one. Finally stylistic criteria were sought, all with the object of defining the precise linguistic environment in which a strictly synchronic description of the words in question could be undertaken.

3. *Semantic universals operate in OT Hebrew as actively as in any other language.* For a number of reasons, theological and cultural, scholars of previous generations had a feeling that Hebrew, and in particular OT Hebrew, exhibited so many unique features that it had to be treated in a way altogether different from, for instance, the Indo-European languages.[3] The backlog of this misapprehension is still present in a good

deal of Semitic and OT research. We have seen how as a religious text, the OT has some distinctive features, and the Semitic languages certainly do have some unique phonological, grammatical and semantic characteristics. But the sum of all these distinguishing features is not so great as the number of features which Hebrew has in common with other languages. Hebrew is just another language, and the application of linguistic universals to Hebrew, although in its infancy, proved rewarding.

4. *A structural approach is required as much for semantic description as for phonological and grammatical analysis.* As a first step in working out such an approach, it was found that the rudiments of transformational grammar can profitably be applied to two important areas of linguistic description. First, in order to explain the relationship between verbal forms like hošia' and hoši'eni and noun-phrases containing the terms yeša', y^ešu'a, etc., it was possible to postulate a single underlying kernel from which all sentences containing any of the *YŠ'-terms are generated according to the appropriate transformational rules. One then has the immediate practical advantage of being able to investigate the incidence of HOŠIA' and the precise relations between it and other lexical items in all the various forms and complex sentences where it occurs. On the other hand transformational analysis unearthed an interesting distinction between HOŠIA' and HIṢṢIL, which has semantic implications: the fact that HOŠIA' has no less than four nominalizations, while HIṢṢIL has none, means that the semantic range of the former is far wider and richer than that of the latter: expressions like koba' y^ešu'a 'the helmet of salvation' and ma'^ayane hay^ešu'a 'the wells of salvation' do not occur with HIṢṢIL.

Two main approaches towards a structural theory of semantics have been put forward in recent years, associated with the names of John Lyons, on the one hand, and Jerrold J. Katz on the other.[4] In *Structural Semantics* (1963) Lyons takes 'meaning-relations' as his model. Incompatibility, antonymy, hyponymy, consequence and synonymy are analysed and the meaning of linguistic items defined without reference to extra-lingual features (reference is a relation of a different kind). In the event, most of these meaning-relations are not contracted by HOŠIAʿ, HIṢṢIL, etc., and the question arises whether a method of semantic analysis designed for the description of part of the vocabulary of Plato is applicable to all linguistic data. One general distinction which did emerge from an analysis of meaning-relations, however, was that HOŠIAʿ contracts relations (poetic parallelism, hyponymy, antonymy) with terms denoting general physical and psychological health, HIṢṢIL with terms denoting movement from one place to another.

The other main approach to semantic theory, 'componential analysis', seeks to identify a set of semantic elements or components. We found it possible, in the present context, to speak of 'an element of separation' common to HOŠIAʿ, HIṢṢIL, etc. Such an element, however, unlike the most often quoted examples, 'Adult', 'Male', etc., is context-bound, and moreover varies in degree from one member of the lexical group to another. It may be that the undoubted contribution of componential analysis to the development of semantics is more readily applicable to some sections of the vocabulary of a language than to others.

5. Finally, *semantic analysis must be monolingual.* In this respect the Hebrew language department in the Hebrew University, Jerusalem, has some advantage over corresponding departments elsewhere. Even although Modern Hebrew is to be carefully distinguished from OT Hebrew, at all levels, phonological, grammatical and semantic, there is inevitably a much wider cultural overlap there than there is between Hebrew and English, or between Hebrew and German. One of the chief obstacles to good semantic theory in much OT scholarship has been the persistent practice of overestimating the importance of English equivalents: dabar means both 'word' and 'thing'; yᵉšuʿa means 'victory' as well as 'salvation'. Only at the very end of the study of the meaning of a given item is it appropriate to suggest English equivalents: only after the semantic description is complete are we ready to contemplate translation.

In the present study, it has been established that HOŠIAʿ has a distinctively religious application not only in Hebrew but in every other language where it occurs. In English 'save' would be the equivalent. To avoid 'save' and 'salvation' because they are 'too pietistic' is to miss the essential distinction between HOŠIA' and the other words in its field. A forensic application is also detectable especially in the expression w^{e}'en mošia' and in this case the English equivalent might be 'and he (she, etc.) had no defence'.

Finally, we come back to where we began, to the role of comparative philology in OT studies. The teaching of Biblical Hebrew is still very often adorned with the Akkadian tense-system, the structure of Arabic nouns and a good deal of comparative Semitic phonology. This method may help and interest some, but it undoubtedly confuses many others at an elementary stage; in any case, it is no more than an 'optional extra', and by no means indispensable for a complete pedagogical description of the language. A similar emphasis is built into our lexica, which tempt even the most circumspect student to begin his research into the meaning of a word with extremely fascinating, but often entirely irrelevant information about similar terms in other Semitic languages. HOŠIA', YEŠA', etc. occur in more than 300 different contexts in the OT, and a detailed analysis of even a few of these turned out to be a very much more arduous task than 'etymologizing', but at the same time very rewarding. The present experiment was intended to show just how much semantic information of various kinds is still available within OT Hebrew.

NOTES

CHAPTER I

1. E.g. W. Schottroff, *'Gedenken' im alten Orient und im Alten Testament. Die Würzel zakar im semitischen Sprachkreis,* Neukirchen-Vluyn, 1964; D. Hill, *Greek Words and Hebrew Meanings,* 1967; W. Eisenbeis, *Die Würzel šlm im Alten Testament* (BZAW 113), 1969; J.R. Wilch, *Time and Event. An exegetical study of the use of 'eth in the Old Testament in comparison to other temporal expressions in clarification of the concept of time*, E.J. Brill, Leiden 1969.

2. J. Barr, *The Semantics of Biblical Language*, 1961 (German translation: *Bibelexegese und moderne Semantik*, Munich 1965; Italian translation: *Semantica del linguaggio biblico*, Bologna 1968).

3. See J. Barr, *Biblical Words for Time*, rev. ed., pp.184-8, 'Further Discussion of Biblical Semantics'.

4. Cf. J. Barr, 'Common Sense and Biblical Language', *Biblica* 49, 1968, pp.377-8 (review of Hill, op. cit.).

5. E.g. J. Barr, 'The Image of God in the Book of Genesis: a Study in Terminology', *Bulletin of the John Rylands Library* 51, 1968, pp.11-26; J.F.A. Sawyer, 'Root-meanings in Hebrew', *JSS* 12, 1967, pp. 43-6; id., 'Spaciousness. An Important Feature of Language about Salvation in the Old Testament', *ASTI* 6, 1968, pp. 20-34.

6. E.g. Hill, op. cit., pp.4ff. and 18ff.

7. E.g. H. Kosmala, 'The Term GEBER in the Old Testament and in the Scrolls', *Congress Volume, Rome 1968, SVT* 17, 1969, pp. 159-69.

CHAPTER II

1. S. Mowinckel, *He that Cometh,* Blackwell 1959, p.69 (*Han som kommer,* Copenhagen 1951).

2. A. Schultens, *Origines Hebraeae,* p.81; cf. BDB, KB; *TWNT* VII, 1964, pp.973f.; W.R. Harper, *Amos and Hosea,* p.205; S.R. Driver, *Notes on the Hebrew Text of Samuel,* pp.118f: H.-J. Kraus, *Psalmen,* p.26; J.

Pedersen, *Israel. Its Life and Culture* I-II, Oxford University Press 1926, pp.330ff.; Mowinckel, op. cit., p.47; E.M.B. Green, *The Meaning of Salvation*, Hodder & Stoughton 1965, p.15.

3. See below, pp.93ff.

4. Cf. BH^3, JB and NEB; Harper, op. cit., pp.180f.; R.S. Cripps, *Amos*, p.241.

5. The term is first used in this sense by M.A.K. Halliday: see n.10 below.

6. H. Gunkel, 'Grundprobleme der israelitischen Literaturgeschichte', *DLZ* 27, 1906, pp.29-38; cf. K. Koch, *The Growth of Biblical Tradition*, esp. pp.26ff.; J. Muilenberg, 'The Gains of Form-criticism in Old Testament Studies', *ExpT* 71, 1959-60, pp.229-33.

7. B. Malinowski, 'The Problem of Meaning in Primitive Languages'; J.R. Firth, *Papers in Linguistics, 1934-1951;* J. Ellis, 'On Contextual Meaning', *In Memory of J.R. Firth*, pp.79-95. Cf. J.F.A. Sawyer, 'Context of Situation and *Sitz im Leben*', pp.137ff.

8. *The New English Bible*, with the Apocrypha, Oxford University Press 1970, p.xviii.

9. Cf. J.F.A. Sawyer, 'An Analysis of the Context and Meaning of the Psalm-headings', *TGUOS* 22, 1967-68, pp.26-38. Similar interest in the final form of the Psalms was shown by B.S. Childs and F.F. Bruce at recent meetings of the Society for Old Testament Study.

10. M.A.K. Halliday, *The Language of the Chinese 'Secret History of the Mongols'* (Publications of the Philological Society 17), 1959, pp.13-24.

11. The term was used by N.W. Porteous in a paper read to the summer meeting of the Society for Old Testament Study in York, 1967.

12. B.S. Childs, *Isaiah and the Assyrian Crisis*, p.121.

13. Ibid., p.127.

14. I.T. Ramsey, *Religious Language. An Empirical Placing of Theological Phrases*, SCM Press 1957, pp.11-48.

15. G. von Rad, *Genesis*, p.27.

16. Cf. J. Lyons, *Introduction to Theoretical Linguistics*, p.2; H.M. Hoenigswald, 'A Proposal for the Study of Folk-linguistics', pp.17,20.

17. See below, p.94.

18. Cf. J. Barr, 'Common Sense and Biblical Language', *Biblica* 49, 1968, pp.387f.

19. M. Noth, *Exodus*, p.18.

20. See above, p.6.

21. Cf. J.H. Eaton, 'The Origin of the Book of Isaiah', *VT* 9, 1959, p.138-57.

22. Cf. Childs, op. cit., p.124.

23. For this translation see the article referred to in n.9 above, pp.32f.

24. C.A. Briggs and E.G. Briggs, *The Book of Psalms* II, pp.4, 458.

25. Cf. A. Weiser, *The Psalms*, pp.401f.,764, but see Kraus, *Psalmen*, p.385.

26. Cf. G. von Rad, *Old Testament Theology* I, pp.398ff.

27. See below, p.22.

28. Cf. GK, p.103 n.1; BL, p.506; KB, p.805.

29. See BDB, p.200. Cf. H. Gese, 'Kleine Beiträge zum Verständnis des Amosbuches', *VT* 12, 1962, pp.427ff.

30. G. Stričević, 'Drama as an Intermediary between Scripture and Byzantine Painting', *Stil und Überlieferung in der Kunst des Abendlandes* I, Bonn 1967, pp.106-27.

31. Ibid., p.109.

32. Weiser, *Psalms*, p.724; von Rad, op. cit., p.400; B.S. Childs, *Memory and Tradition* pp.81-9; N.W. Porteous, 'Actualization and the Prophetic Criticism of the Cult', *Living the Mystery*, Blackwell 1967 (reprinted from *Tradition und Situation. Studien zum ATlichen Prophetie. Artur Weiser zum 70. Geburtstage dargebracht*, Göttingen 1963).

33. Childs, op. cit., p.34.

34. Koch cites a few examples: op. cit., pp.15f. On stylistics in general, see N.E. Enkvist and others, *Linguistics and Style.*

35. GK, pp.13-15.

36. Cf. J. Skinner, *Genesis*, pp.xviii-xx.

37. BDB, p.609, s.v. -na, 1.

38. For the terminology, see M.A.K. Halliday and others, *The Linguistic Sciences and Language Teaching*, pp.87-94.

39. G. von Rad, *Deuteronomy*, p.49.

40. Weiser, *Psalms*, p.618.

41. H.S. Nyberg, 'Smärtornas man. En studie till Jes. 52,13-53,12', *Svensk Exegetisk Årsbok* 7, 1948, p.48; GK 144p.

42. Cf. G.R. Driver, *Canaanite Myths and Legends*, p.132; E. Ullendorff, *The Challenge of Amharic*, University of London. 1965, pp.7f.

43. Cf. C.R. North, *The Second Isaiah*, pp.6ff.; R.B.Y. Scott, 'The Literary Structure of Isaiah's Oracles', *Studies in Old Testament Prophecy*, ed. H.H. Rowley, T. and T. Clark 1950, pp.183-6.

44. See below, p.22.

45. E.g. C. Westermann, 'Struktur und Geschichte der Klage im Alten Testament', *ZAW* 66, 1954, pp.44-60; B. Hornig, 'Das Prosagebet der nachexilischen Literatur', *TLZ* 83, 1958, cols. 644-6: O. Eissfeldt, *The Old Testament. An Introduction*, pp.17f.

46. E.g. *TDNT* II, p.785; W. Eichrodt, *Theology of the Old Testament* I, p.172.

47. Ex. 32.11-13; Deut. 3.24f.; Jer. 31.18f.; Judg. 13.8; Job 7.12-21; 10.2-22.

48. Enkvist and others, op. cit., p. 28. This stylistic section is documented more fully in the original thesis (see preface, p.vii) and is to be published separately in full.

49. The three short prayers of Elisha in II Kings 6 are exceptional, and serve to emphasize the consistency of all the others. On Jonah 2 see pp.13f.

50. E.g. 400 prophets (I Kings 22), Micaiah Ben Imlah (loc. cit.), and Elisha (II Kings 8).

51. Cf. H. Gunkel, *Genesis*, p.358, where a feature termed *Näherbestimmung* is discussed.

52. Gen. 3.10,12f.; 4.9,13; 15.2f.,8; 17.17f.; 18.3-5,23-33; 19.2,18-20;

20.4f.; 22.1-11; 31.11; 32.26ff.; 46.2; Ex. 3.11,13; 4.1,10; 5.22f.; 6.30; 19.23; 33.12f.,15f.,18; Num. 11.11-15,21-22; 16.15; 22.10f.,34; 27.16f.; Judg. 6.13,15,17,22,36f.,39; 13.11f.,15,17; I Kings 19.10 = 14; Isa. 40.6; Jer. 1.6,11,13; 4.10; 14.13; Ezek. 21.5; 37.3; Zech. 1.9,12,19,21; 2.2; 4.2-4,11-13; 5.2,6,10; 6.4; Mal. 1.2,6f.; 3.13; Job 1.7,9-11; 2.2,4f.; 42.2-6; Dan. 12.6,8.

53. Ex. 34.8-9; Num. 10.35,36; 16.22; Deut. 26.13-15; Josh. 7.7-9; Judg. 21.3; I Sam. 3.9f.; 14.41; 23.10-12; II Sam. 24.10,17=I Chron. 21.8,17; I Kings 3.6-9 = II Chron. 1.8-10; I Kings 8.13 = II Chron. 6.1; I Kings 18.36f.; Isa. 6.8,11; 44.17; Jer. 2.27; 51.62; Joel 2.17; Lam. 3.42-66; I Chron. 16.35 = Ps. 106.47; I Chron. 29.10-19; II Chron. 20.6-12.

54. Gen. 24.12-14; 32.9-13; Ex. 32.31f.; Num. 14.13-19; I Kings 19.4; Isa. 12; Hos. 2.25; 14.2f.; Amos 7.2,5.

55. Isa. 25.1-5; 33.2-4; 63.7-64.11; Jer. 3.22-25; 5.3; 10.6f.,23-25; 11.18-20; 12.1-4; 14.7-9,19-22; 15.15-18; 16.19; 17.13-18; 18.19-23; 20.7-18; Hos. 9.14; Joel 1.19f.; Micah 7.14-20; Hab. 1.2-4,12-14; Lam. 1.9,11,20-22; 2.20-22; 5.1-22; Job 9.25-31; 13.18-4.22; 30.23; Neh. 3.36f.; 5.19; 6.14; 13.14,22,29,31.

56. The Psalms, most of which (apart from the 'Songs of the Temple-steps', Pss. 120-134) contain language addressed to God, raise peculiar problems as regards their context and style, and are best dealt with on their own. See Sawyer, 'Psalm-headings'.

CHAPTER III

1. Cf. N. Chomsky, *Current Issues in Linguistic Theory*, p.52.

2. S. Ullmann, *Language and Style*, 1964; see also the same author's *The Principles of Semantics*, 1957, and *Semantics. An Introduction to the Science of Meaning*, 1962.

3. H. Kronasser, *Handbuch der Semasiologie*, 1952; P. Guiraud, *La Sémantique*, 1955; E. Struck, *Bedeutungslehre. Grundzüge einer lateinischen und griechischen Semasiologie*, Stuttgart 1954.

4. 'Componential analysis', another lexicon-based approach, will be discussed on pp.121,126.

5. J. Lyons, *Structural Semantics*. 1963, cf. his *Introduction to Theoretical Linguistics*, pp.443-70.

6. Cf. J. McH. Sinclair, 'Beginning the Study of Lexis', *In Memory of J.R. Firth*, pp.410-30; J.R. Firth, *Papers in Linguistics 1934-1951*, pp.194-6; M.A.K. Halliday and others, *The Linguistic Sciences and Language Teaching*, pp.33-5; J. Ellis, 'On Contextual Meaning', *In Memory of J.R. Firth*, pp.79-95; W.M. Urban, *Language and Reality*, 1939; P. Ziff, *Semantic Analysis*, 1960.

7. Cf. Ullmann, *Language and Style*, pp.63-96, where references to 'universals' in the writings of Jespersen, Bloomfield and others are given.

8. See below, p.57, on 'interference'.

9. Lyons, op. cit., pp.74-8.

10. Cf. F. de Saussure, *Course in General Linguistics*, pp.134f.

11. This is the shorthand formula for describing a lexical group. Cf. p.31.

12. J. Trier, *Der Deutsche Wortschatz im Sinnbezirk des Verstandes*, 1931.

13. See for example S. Öhmann, 'Theories of the "Linguistic Field"', N.C.W. Spence, 'Linguistic Fields, Conceptual Spheres and the *Weltbild'*, *Transactions of the Philological Society*, 1961, pp.87-106; Lyons, *Introduction*, pp.429ff.

14. Cf. C. Rabin, 'Is Biblical Semantics Possible?', p.22 n.24.

15. De Saussure, op. cit., p.1.

16. Ch. Bally, 'L'arbitraire du signe', *Le français moderne* 8, 1940, p.195.

17. Cf. Ullmann, op. cit., p.11.

18. E.g. BDB, p.446.

19. W. Schottroff, *'Gedenken'*, see ch.I n.1 above; R. Knierim, *Die Hauptbegriffe für Sünde*, Gütersloh 1965.

20. E.g. the section on 'The Political Concept of Freedom in the Greek World' under *ἐλεύθερος* (*TDNT* II, 487ff.), 'The New Testament Concept of Sacrifice and the Early Church' under *θύω* (*TDNT* III, pp.189f.), 'The Concept of Conversion' under *νοέω* (*TDNT* IV, pp.1000-6). Cf. Barr, *Semantics*, p.229, and the present writer's reviews of *TDNT* in the *Scottish Journal of Theology*, 19-24, 1966-71.

21. Knierim, op. cit., p.113.

22. Schottroff, op. cit.; Childs, *Memory and Tradition;* P.A.H. de Boer, *Gedenken und Gedachtnis in der Welt des Alten Testaments*, Stuttgart 1962. Cf. Kraus, *Psalmen*, p.359.

23. J. Barr, *Biblical Words for Time;* A. Schwarzenbach, *Die geographische Terminologie im Alten Testament*, Leiden 1954; A.M. Honeyman, 'The pottery vessels in the Old Testament', *PEQ* 71, 1939, pp.76-90. Cf. Rabin, op. cit., p.22.

24. P. Guiraud, 'Les champs morpho-sémantiques', *Bulletin de la société de linguistique de Paris* 52, 1956, pp.265-88.

25. Cf. H.L. Strack, *Hebräisches Vokabularium in grammatischer und sachlicher Ordnung*, 12th ed., revised by A. Jepsen, Munich 1929; H. Weinheimer, *Hebräisches Wörterbuch in sachlicher Ordnung*, Tübingen 1918.

26. Cf. H.A. Gleason, *Descriptive Linguistics*, p.186; Ziff, op. cit., pp.9f; Lyons, *Structural Semantics*, pp.94-9; id., *Introduction*, p. 154

27. Ziff, op. cit., p.41.

28. See Sawyer, 'Spaciousness'.

29. E.g. Pss. 4.2 (EVV 4.1); 18.20 (EVV 18.19); 31.9 (EVV 31.8); 118.5; Job 36.16.

30. See pp.57f.

31. See p.95.

32. KB, p.772; M. Wagner, *Aramäismen*, p.94.

33. Cf. Ps. 105.20.

34. Kronasser, *Handbuch*, p.142; E. Haugen, 'The Analysis of Linguis-

tic Borrowing', *Language* 26, 1950, p.228; T.E. Hope, 'The Analysis of Semantic Borrowing', pp.133f.; cf. Weinreich, *Languages in Contact.* pp.56ff.

35. Cf. BH^3; RSV, NEB, JB: Kraus, *Psalmen,* p.489; Weiser, *Psalms,* p.495.

36. Cf. Ps. 106.4. Whether divine intervention in this case refers to the sending of commissioned deputies or angels (Ibn Ezra, Rashi) is not specified.

37. KB; BH^3; Kraus, op. cit., p.489; BDB; Weiser, op. cit., p.496. Cf. RSV.

38. Cf. Kronasser, *Handbuch,* p.140; and on the suggestion that Semitic *DYN 'to judge' is another example (cf. Egyptian dn 'to cut'), see W.A. Ward, 'Comparative studies in Egyptian and Ugaritic', *JNES* 20, 1961, p.33.

39. This is apparently how the word was understood in antiquity: cf. LXX σκεπαστής; Vulgate *protector.* The emendations ʿezrati or ʿuzzi are unnecessary: *difficilior lectio potior est.*

40. Cf. BH^3; *Biblica Hebraica Stuttgartensia. Jesaia* (ed. D. Winton Thomas, 1968); NEB.

41. Cf. KB 'to get through with bread' (Gen. 47.17); Skinner, *Genesis,* pp.499f.; von Rad, *Genesis,* p.404.

42. The evidence for Proto-Semitic *NWḤ is good (Ugaritic, Akkadian, Phoenician, Aramaic, Arabic, Ethiopic); but the evidence for a separate root *NḤW/Y, from which Hebrew NAḤA is derived, is less impressive (KB, p.606).

43. B. Duhm, *Psalmen,* 2nd ed., Tubingen 1922, p.17; J. Ziegler, 'Die Hilfe Gottes "am Morgen"', *Nötscher Festschrift,* edd. H. Junker and J. Botterweck, Bonn 1950, pp.281-8. Cf. RSV.

44. See D. Hill, *Greek Words and Hebrew Meanings,* pp.8-14, for a sympathetic reappraisal of the effects of neo-Humboldtian linguistics and the Sapir-Whorf hypothesis on biblical scholarship. Contrast J. Barr, *Semantics,* pp. 33-45.

45. Hill, op. cit., p.294. Cf. Barr, op. cit., pp.282-7.

46. E. Ullendorff, 'Is Biblical Hebrew a Language?' *BSOAS* 34, pp.249ff.

47. Cf. H.H. Rowley, 'Moses and Monotheism', *From Moses to Qumran,* Lutterworth 1963, pp.48ff. (first published in German in *ZAW* 28, 1957, pp.1-21).

48. See above, p.14.

49. H. Sperber, *Einführung in die Bedeutungslehre,* p.67; cf. Ullmann, *Language and Style,* p.83; and see below, p.54.

50. See below, pp.99-101.

51. Cf. Ullmann, op. cit., p.75. He quotes examples from *Beowulf* and Benoît de Sainte-Maure.

52. See pp.53f.

53. Cf. Ps. 30.2 (EVV 30.1).

54. See pp.54f.

55. See pp.100f.

56. Cf. Kraus, *Psalmen,* p.586. He cites a parallel from the Amarna

letters.

57. See Sawyer, 'Spaciousness', pp.26ff.

58. Cf. von Rad, *Old Testament Theology* I, pp.368f., 395ff.; Weiser, *Psalms,* p.39; Childs, *Memory and Tradition*, p.37.

59. Kraus, *Psalmen,* p.509. Cf. Isa. 45.1, on which see C. Westermann, *Isaiah 40-66*, p.158.

60. Kraus, *Psalmen*, p.807.

61. Cf. I. Engnell, *Studies in Divine Kingship,* 2nd ed., Oxford 1967, pp.35f.; D.R. Jones, 'Isaiah II and III', *Peake's Commentary on the Bible*, edd. M. Black and H.H. Rowley, Nelson 1962, p.525; *ANET*, p.334.

62. A.R. Johnson, 'The Psalms', *The Old Testament and Modern Study*, ed. H.H. Rowley, Clarendon Press 1951, p.204; H. Ringgren, *Israelite Religion,* SPCK 1966, pp.183f. (*Israelitische Religion,* Stuttgart 1963); H.-J. Kraus, *Worship in Israel. A Cultic History of the Old Testament,* Blackwell 1966, pp.14-19 (*Gottesdienst in Israel,* Munich 1962).

63. B. Albrektson, *History and the Gods. An Essay on the Idea of Historical Events as Divine Manifestations in the Ancient Near East and in Israel* (Coniectanea Biblica, Old Testament Series, 1), Lund 1967, pp.113f.

64. Cf. Kraus, *Psalmen,* p.91; and on Gen. 44.5, see H. Gunkel, *Genesis,* pp.453f.; von Rad, *Genesis,* p.387. See also A. Jirku, 'Mantik in Alt Israel', *Von Jerusalem nach Ugarit. Gesammelte Studien,* Graz 1966, pp.161f.

65. For ʿALA 'to go up' as a technical term, see Kraus, *Psalmen*, p.196; S. Mowinckel, *The Psalms in Israel's Worship,* I, pp.178f.

66. See above.

67. See for example S.G.F. Brandon, ed., *The Saviour God. Comparative Studies in the Concept of Salvation presented to E.O. James,* Oxford University Press 1963; E.M.B. Green, *The Meaning of Salvation,* Hodder & Stoughton 1965; S. Porubčan, *Sin in the Old Testament. A Soteriological Study*, Rome 1963.

68. See p.79.

69. Cf. H.-J. Kraus, *Threni*, pp.74f.

70. Cf. C.R. North, *The Second Isaiah*, p.179.

71. Cf. S.R. Driver, *The Book of Daniel,* Cambridge University Press 1900, pp.190-3; N.W. Porteous, *Daniel*, p.168.

72. Cf. S.R. Driver and G.B. Gray, *The Book of Job*, p.74.

73. Cf. W.R. Harper, *Amos and Hosea*, p.10; R.S. Cripps, *Amos*, p.115. On 'the prophet's freedom' in general, see G. von Rad, *Old Testament Theology* II, pp.70-9.

74. For the lack of distinction in Hebrew between qualitative and quantitative, see C. Rabin, 'Is Biblical Semantics Possible?', pp.22f. Cf. Jer. 45.3; Prov. 14.13 (cf. Arabic ka'iba 'to be sad'); Jer. 3.22; 14.19; 17.14; 30.17.

75. Cf. D.R. Jones, 'Isaiah II and III', op. cit., p.525.

76. But see J. Skinner, *Isaiah XL-LXVI*, Cambridge University Press 1902, p.125; North, op. cit., p.237; and NEB 'health' for ŠALOM in 53.5.

77. Cf. von Rad, *Old Testament Theology* II, pp.258-62; Westermann, *Isaiah 40-66*, pp.20f.; P.R. Ackroyd, *Exile and Restoration*, SCM Press 1968, pp.126-8.

78. E. Jenni, *Das hebräische Pi'el. Syntaktische-semasiologische Untersuchung einer Verbalform im Alten Testament*, Zürich 1968; Sawyer, 'Root-meanings in Hebrew', *JSS* 12, pp.37-50.

79. Cf. S. Ullmann's 'semantic universals', op. cit., pp.63-96.

80. Ibid., pp.40-9; cf. 'Root-meanings', pp.38-40.

81. See below, p.94.

82. 'Root-meanings', pp.39f.

83. Ullmann, op. cit., p.68.

84. *Textbook*, pp.84f. cf. R. Pines, The Problem of Indeterminacy in Unvocalized Hebrew Spelling (Dissertation, Hebrew University, 1965).

85. Ullmann, op. cit., pp.55-7; H.A. Gleason, *Descriptive Linguistics*, p.436. On homonyms in the OT, see J. Barr, *Comparative Philology*, pp.125-55.

86. Cf. Harper, *Amos and Hosea*, p.240; Wolff, *Hosea*, p.53. BDB translates 'sing'; cf. AV. RSV has 'answer'; BH^3 and KB emend the text.

87. C.H. Gordon, *Ugaritic Textbook*, Glossary no.1885; cf. J. Aistleitner, *Wörterbuch*, p.237 (2060, 9*b).

88. Cf. J. Hempel, 'Jahwegleichnisse der Propheten', *ZAW* 42, 1924, pp.74-104; W. Eichrodt, *Theology of the Old Testament* I, pp.211f.

89. E.g. Judg. 7.2; II Kings 16.7.

90. Cf. L. Bloomfield, *Language*, p.429.

91. See above p.41.

92. See pp.94f.

93. See Table 2 on p.37.

94. See pp.94f.

95. Cf. C. Rabin, *millim zarot* ('Foreign Words'), *Encyclopaedia Biblica* IV, Jerusalem 1962, cols. 1070-80; 'Hittite Words in Hebrew', *Orientalia* 32, 1963, pp.113-39; Wagner, *Aramaismen*, 1966.

96. T.E. Hope, *Archivum Linguisticum* 14, 1962, pp.111-21; 15, 1963, pp.29-42.

97. Wagner, op. cit., p.97; cf. also BL, p.24 and KB, p.8.

98. Cf. Sawyer, 'Root-meanings', p.42.

99. Cf. Th. C. Vriezen, *An Outline of Old Testament Theology*, Blackwell 1960, p.232.

100. Ullman, op. cit., p.12. Cf. Weinreich, *Languages in Contact*, *passim*.

101. S. Moscati, ed., *Comparative Grammar*, p.75.

102. Briggs, *Psalms* I, p.374.

103. E.g. Judg. 2.16,18, corresponding to 3.9,15. See C.F. Burney, *The Book of Judges*, pp.xxxiii note and p.59.

104. Cf. RSV, following LXX and Peshitta; A.F. Kirkpatrick, *The Book of Psalms*, Cambridge University Press 1903, p.120; Briggs, op. cit., I, p.205; Kraus, *Psalmen*, p.176.

105. Literally, 'You have spoken up in my defence'. Cf. Weiser, *Psalms*, p.218, who gives the translation 'rescue', without taking 'ANA as a

forensic term.

106. Lyons, *Introduction*, pp.470-80; J.J. Katz, *The Philosophy of Language*, esp. pp.151-8, 240-82.

107. See note 78 above.

108. See pp.

109. It is readily applicable to kinship terms, for example: cf. W.H. Goodenough, 'Componential Analysis and the Study of Meaning', *Language* 32, 1956, pp.195-216; F.C. Wallace and J. Atkins, 'The Meaning of Kinship Terms', *American Anthropologist* 62, 1960, pp.58-80.

110. Cf. Lyons, *Introduction*, pp.480f.

CHAPTER IV

1. Cf.p.49.

2. Cf. Lyons, *Structural Semantics*, pp.95ff.

3. See Table 1 on p.27.

4. For useful introductory material, see Lyons, *Introduction*, pp.247-69; id., *Chomsky*, pp.66-82; and the other modern introductions listed in the bibliography.

5. Lexemes in the underlying structure are printed in capitals, surface-structure (i.e. masoretic text) in lower case.

6. See p.72.

7. Cf. Deut. 33.7; I Sam. 2.1; II Sam. 22.42; Isa. 12.3; Jonah 2.10; Hab. 3.8; Lam. 2.8. Deletion of the subject occurs only in Lam. 2.22.

8. GK, 128q, J. Skinner, *Isaiah XL-LXVI*, Cambridge University Press 1902, p.127, and G.A.F. Knight, *Deutero-Isaiah*, New York 1965, pp.233-5, favour the former; RSV, A. Simon, *A Theology of Salvation*, SPCK 1953, pp.210-14, C.R. North, *The Second Isaiah*, pp.239f. and C. Westermann, *Isaiah 40-66*, p.263, favour the latter. NEB and JB have present tenses.

9. Lyons, *Structural Semantics*, pp.117f.

10. H.A. Sweet, *A New English Grammar*, para. 58.

11. H.A. Gleason, *Descriptive Linguistics*, p.156.

12. Ps. 132.9: see Weiser, *Psalms*, p.781; Kraus, *Psalmen*, p.877.

13. Deut. 33.29b; II Sam. 22.3b,36,47; Isa. 12.2a,3; Hab. 3.18; I Chron. 16.35. mark^{e}boteka y^{e}šu'a 'your chariots of salvation' (Hab. 3.8) has parallels in the OT and emendation is unnecessary: cf. GK, 131r; C. Brockelmann, *Hebräische Syntax*, para. 81c. BH^{3} emends the text; cf. F. Horst ad loc. in *Nahum bis Maleachi* (HAT 14), 3rd ed., 1964, p.182.

14. Cf. Brockelmann, op. cit., para. 47; GK, 114i; BH^{3}.

15. Cf. GK, 121f.

16. E.g. Isa. 12.2; Pss. 13.6; 78.22; 86.2; 119.41-2. Cf. Ps. 28.7-9.

17. GK, 119i.

18. For the term 'prepositional verb' (applied to English grammar), see B. Strang, *Modern English Structure*, pp. 177f.

19. Lyons, *Structural Semantics*, p.128.

20. See Table 1 on p.27.

21. See below, pp.71,81.
22. Firth, *Papers in Linguistics*, p.196.
23. Strang, op. cit., pp.85f.
24. Lyons, *Introduction*, p.366.
25. See above, p.64.
26. Cf. BDB, p.446, where II Sam. 14.4 and II Kings 6.26 are cited as examples of intransitive usage.
27. See Table 4 on p.73.
28. Componential analysis is discussed on pp.58f.
29. See Table 4 on p.73. These meaning-relations are discussed in greater detail on pp.72ff.
30. On 'simple' and 'complex' relations see p.74.
31. Lyons, *Structural Semantics*, p.59.
32. Lyons, op. cit., p.41.
33. E.g. E.A. Nida, *Morphology. A Descriptive Analysis of Words*, 2nd ed., Michigan 1949, p.151.
34. Cf. Briggs, *Psalms* I, pp.xxxiv-xlviii; K. Koch, *The Growth of the Biblical Tradition*, pp.92ff.
35. See especially Briggs, loc. cit., and S.R. Driver, *Introduction*, pp.362ff.
36. B.M.G. Reardon, *Religious Thought in the Nineteenth Century*, Cambridge University Press 1966, p.5.
37. Cf. Lyons, *Introduction*, p.427.
38. Lyons, *Structural Semantics*, pp.69-71; *Introduction*, pp.453-60.
39. Lyons, *Introduction*, pp.424ff.
40. M.A.K. Halliday and others, *Linguistic Science*, p.33; J.R. Firth, *Papers in Linguistics*, p.196; D. Crystal, *Linguistics*, pp.87-9.
41. See pp.97f.
42. Cf. Kraus, *Psalmen*, pp.82f.
43. The syntax is difficult, but not 'unverständlich" (W. Rudolph, *Jeremia*, p.26). The oppositions are not in doubt. For g^{e}ba'ot denoting heathen sanctuaries, cf. Deut. 12.2; I Kings 14.23; II Kings 17.10.
44. Cf. Isa. 38.20; I Chron. 16.35.
45. E.g. I Sam. 2.2; II Sam. 7.22; Jonah 4.2; and without ki Dan. 9.4; Ezra 9.14; Neh. 1.5.
46. Cf. North, *The Second Isaiah*, pp.93,208f.; D. Hill, *Greek Words and Hebrew Meanings*, pp.86-92,97f.
47. The relation is a complex one (cf. pp.74f). Duhm's emendation toḥalti 'my hope', which fits the lament-form better and is recommended by Rudolph (*Jeremia*, p.106; cf. BH^{3}), is unnecessary. Cf. Ps. 109.1.
48. Cf. II Chron. 20.19.
49. See above, p.71.
50. On the occurrence of 'ANA in the HOŠIA'-field, see pp.57ff. Cf. Hertzberg, *I and II Samuel* (OTL), 1964, p.390. Other suggestions are to emend the text (BH^{3}), or take the word in the sense 'dein Antworten, dein Orakel' (Kraus, *Psalmen*, p.139).
51. J.F.A. Sawyer, 'What was a Mošia'?', p.482.

CHAPTER V

1. See above, p.29.

2. Barr, *Semantics*, pp.107ff.

3. Cf. Sawyer, 'Psalm-headings', pp.31-3, and H. Gese, 'Kleine Beiträge zum Verständnis des Amosbuches', *VT* 12, 1962, pp.427ff.

4. Aquila; cf. Syro-Hexaplar.

5. See above, pp.14f.

6. Sawyer, 'What was a Mošiaʿ?', pp.485f.

7. The standard comparative grammars and lexica are listed in the bibliography, and are not normally cited.

8. Cf. A. Meillet and M. Cohen, *Les Langues du Monde*, 2nd ed., Paris 1952; M. Cohen, *Essai comparatif sur le vocabulaire et la phonétique du Chamito-Sémitique*, Paris 1947. See also the essay by B.S.J. Isserlin in the forthcoming proceedings of a recent conference on Hamito-Semitic Comparative Linguistics (Janua Linguarum, The Hague).

9. As well as Barr's various publications, see also L. Kopf, 'Das arabische Wörterbuch als Hilfsmittel für die hebräische Lexicographie', *VT* 6, 1956, pp.286-302; R. Katičić, *A Contribution to the General Theory of Comparative Linguistics* (Janua Linguarum, Series Minor, 83), 1970; E.Y. Kutscher, 'Contemporary Studies in North Western Semitic', *JSS* 10, 1965, pp.21-51; M.H. Pope, 'Marginalia to M. Dahood's *Ugaritic-Hebrew philology*' *JBL* 85, 1966, pp.455-66; E. Ullendorff, 'The Contribution of South Semitics to Hebrew Lexicography', *VT* 6, 1956, pp.190-8.

10. Cf. G.R. Driver, *Canaanite Myths and Legends*, p.128.

11. For a detailed historical description of the Hebrew root *YŠʿ, see my paper in the Janua Linguarum volume referred to in n.8 above.

12. Cf. n.10 above.

13. J.A. Knudtzon, *Amarna-Tafeln* II, p.1319.

14. D.D. Luckenbill, *Ancient Records* II, pp.7f.

15. H.B. Huffmon, *Amorite Personal Names*, p.302; F. Gröndahl, *Personennamen*, p.14, para. 13; I.J. Gelb, 'La lingua degli Amoriti', 2.7.3; G. Buccellati, *Amorites*, p.165.

16. Sawyer 'What was a Mosia ?', pp.476-8.

17. Ibid., p.486; W. McKane, *Proverbs*, p.548 (on Prov. 20.22).

18. J.A. Montgomery and H.S. Gehman, *Kings*, p.396. Cf. II Sam. 14.4; II Kings 6.26.

19. See above, p.31.

20. Cf. Skinner, *Genesis*, p.527; G. von Rad, *Genesis*, p.422.

21. nḏ 'to defend, rescue' is attested from the Pyramid Texts onwards.

22. Sawyer, 'What was a Mošiaʿ?' p.479.

23. D. Daube, *The Exodus Pattern in the Bible*, Faber and Faber, 1963, pp.67-72.

24. C.-F. Jean and J. Hoftijzer, *Dictionnaire des inscriptions sémitiques de l'ouest*, pp.185,233.

25. The sign which is transcribed ḏ by Gordon, is transcribed š̲$_2$ by Aistleitner, ž̲ by Driver and ś̲ in Koehler-Baumgartner. But there is no disagreement about Ugaritic ‘ḏr ‘to save, help’.

26. See above, p.92.

27. Cf. Aqhat, III.vi.11 (Driver, *Canaanite Myths and Legends*, p.57).

28. Ugaritic pl̲t̲ occurs in the same context as ‘ḏr (see previous note).

29. See above, pp.41f.

30. See Table 1, p.27.

31. Cf. the accident that ‘aṭiša ‘sneezing’ occurs only once in the OT (Job 41.10). See further R. Lowth, *Isaiah. A new translation with a preliminary dissertation and notes, critical, philological and explanatory*, London 1778, pp.xxxix-xl; Bauer-Leander, section 2r, p.26; E. Ullendorff, ‘Is Biblical Hebrew a Language?’

32. Moscati, ed., *Comparative Grammar*, p.73.

33. See above, p.36.

34. Cf. Briggs, *Psalms*, II, p.520; Weiser, *Psalms*, pp.823f.; Kraus, *Psalmen*, p.942.

CHAPTER VI

1. On the difficulty of distinguishing transitivity in nominalization, see pp.63f.

2. Bibliographical material is listed on pp.130-6 and not repeated here.

CHAPTER VII

1. Cf. A. Jepsen, ‘The scientific study of the Old Testament’, *Essays on Old Testament Interpretation*, ed. C. Westermann, SCM Press 1963, p.255 (*Probleme alttestamentlicher Hermeneutik*, Munich 1960); J. Bright, *The Authority of the Old Testament*, SCM Press 1967, p.169; D. Hill, *Greek Words and Hebrew Meanings*, pp.18f.

2. Cf. E. Ullendorff, ‘Is Biblical Hebrew a Language?’. See also p.99 above.

3. E.g. J.G. Herder, *The Spirit of Hebrew Poetry*, quoted by Barr, *Semantics*, pp.85f.; T. Boman, *Hebrew Thought Compared with Greek*, SCM Press 1960, pp.144f.

4. Lyons, *Structural Semantics*, 1963; Katz, *The Philosophy of Language*, 1966.

BIBLIOGRAPHY

Barr, J., *The Semantics of Biblical Language,* Oxford University Press 1961

– *Biblical Words for Time* (SBT 33) rev. ed. 1969, pp.185-207

–*Comparative Philology and the Text of the Old Testament,* Oxford University Press 1968

Bazell, C.E., Catford, J.C., Halliday, M.A.K., and Robins, R.H., edd., *In Memory of J.R. Firth,* Longmans 1966

Bloomfield, L., *Language,* Allen and Unwin 1935

Catford, J.C., *A Linguistic Theory of Translation,* Oxford University Press 1965

Chomsky, N., *Current Issues in Linguistic Theory* (Janua Linguarum, Series Minor, 38), The Hague 1964

– *Aspects of the Theory of Syntax,* Cambridge, Mass., 1965

– *Linguistics,* Penguin Books 1971

Ellis, J., 'On contextual meaning', *In Memory of J.R. Firth,* ed. C.E. Bazell and others, 1966, pp.79-95

Enkvist, N.E., Spencer, J., and Gregory, M.J., *Linguistics and Style,* Oxford University Press 1964

Firth, J.R., *Papers in Linguistics 1934-1951,* Oxford University Press 1951

Gleason, H.A., *An Introduction to Descriptive Linguistics,* 2nd ed., Holt, Rinehart and Winston 1961

Guiraud, P., *La Sémantique,* Paris 1955

Halliday, M.A.K., McIntosh, A. and Strevens, P.D., *The Linguistic Sciences and Language Teaching,* Longmans 1964

Harris, Z.S., *Structural Linguistics,* University of Chicago Press 1951 (originally entitled *Methods in Structural Linguistics*).

Hill, D.W., *Greek Words and Hebrew Meanings. Studies in the Semantics of Soteriological terms,* Cambridge University Press 1967.

Hoenigswald, H.M., 'A Proposal for the Study of Folk-linguistics', *Socio-linguistics,* ed. W. Bright, The Hague 1966

Hope, T.E., 'The Analysis of Semantic Borrowing', *Essays presented to*

C.M. Girdlestone, Newcastle upon Tyne 1961, pp.123-41

Hymes, D., ed., *Language in Culture and Society: A Reader in Linguistics and Anthropology*, Harper and Row 1964

Jespersen, O., *Language, Its Nature, Development and Origin*, Allen and Unwin 1929

Katičić, R., *A Contribution to The General Theory of Comparative Linguistics*, (Janua Linguarum, Series Minor, 83), The Hague 1970

Katz, J.J., *The Philosophy of Language*, Harper and Row 1966

Kronasser H., *Handbuch der Semasiologie*, Heidelberg 1952

Lyons, J., *Structural Semantics* (Publications of the Philological Society 20), Blackwell 1963

– *Introduction to Theoretical Linguistics*, Cambridge University Press 1968

–*Chomsky* (Fontana Modern Masters, ed. F. Kermode), Collins 1970

Malinowski, B., 'The Problem of Meaning in Primitive Languages', Supplement I to Ogden and Richards *The Meaning of Meaning*, pp.296-346

Nida, E.A., *Towards a Science of Translating*, Leiden 1964

Ogden, C.K., and Richards, I.A., *The Meaning of Meaning*, 8th ed., Routledge and Kegan Paul 1946

Öhmann, S., 'Theories of the "Linguistic Field"', *Word* 9, 1953, pp.123-34

Rabin, C., 'hattitaken semanṭiqa miqraʾit?' ('Is Biblical Semantics Possible?') *Bet-Miqraʾ*, *Quarterly of the Society of Biblical Research in Israel*, Jerusalem 1962, pp.17-27

– ' *ʿibrit*' ('Hebrew'), Encyclopaedia Biblica VI, Jerusalem 1971, cols.51-73

Robins, R.H., *General Linguistics. An Introductory Survey*, Longmans 1964

Saussure, F.de., *Course in General Linguistics*, New York 1959 (*Cours de Linguistique Générale*, 5th ed., Paris 1955)

Sawyer, J.F.A., 'What was a Mošiaʿ?' *VT* 15, 1965, pp.475-86

– 'Root-meanings in Hebrew', *JSS* 12, 1967, pp.37-50

– 'An Analysis of the Context and Meaning of the Psalm-headings' *TGUOS* 22, 1967-8, pp.26-38

– 'Context of Situation and *Sitz im Leben*', *Proceedings of the Newcastle upon Tyne Philosophical Society* 1, 1967, pp.137-47

– 'Spaciousness. An Important Feature of Language about Salvation in the Old Testament' *ASTI* 6, 1968, pp.20-34

– 'The Place of Folk-linguistics in Biblical Interpretation', *Proceedings of the Fifth World Congress of Jewish Studies*, I, 1971

Sperber, H., *Einführung in die Bedeutungslehre*, Bonn 1923

Strang, B., *Modern English Structure*, 2nd ed., Edward Arnold 1969

Sweet, H., *A New English Grammar, Logical and Historical*, Clarendon Press 1891-8

Trier, J., *Der deutsche Wortschatz im Sinnbezirk des Verstandes*, Heidelberg 1931

Ullendorff, E., 'Is Biblical Hebrew a Language?', *BSOAS* 34, 1971,

pp.241-55
Ullmann, S., *The Principles of Semantics*, 2nd ed., Blackwell 1957
– *Semantics. An Introduction to the Science of Meaning*, Blackwell 1962
– *Language and Style*, Blackwell 1964
Urban, W.M., *Language and Reality*, Allen and Unwin 1939
Weinreich, U., *Languages in Contact*, New York 1953
Whorf, B.L., *Language, Thought and Reality: Selected Papers*, ed. J.B. Carroll, New York 1956
Ziff, P., *Semantic Analysis*, Cornell University Press, New York 1960

2. Texts, Commentaries, etc.

Biblia Hebraica, ed. R. Kittel, 7th ed., revised by A. Alt and O. Eissfeldt, Stuttgart 1937
Biblia Hebraica Stuttgartensia, Editio funditus renovata, edd. K. Elliger and W. Rudolph. Fasc.7 *Liber Jesaiae* (ed. D.W. Thomas), 1968
– Fasc.11 *Liber Psalmorum* (ed. H. Bardtke), 1969
Branden, A. van der, *Les Textes Thamoudéens de Philby*, I, Louvain 1956
Briggs, C.A. and E.G., *A Critical and Exegetical Commentary on the Book of Psalms* (ICC), 2 vols., 1906
Buccellati, G., *The Amorites of the Ur III Period*, Naples 1966
Burney, C.A., *The Book of Judges with Introduction and Notes*, London 1918
Charles, R.H., ed., *The Apocrypha and Pseudepigrapha of the Old Testament*, 2 vols., Clarendon Press 1913
Childs, B.S., *Memory and Tradition in Israel*(SBT 37), 1962
– *Isaiah and the Assyrian Crisis* (SBT, second series, 3), 1967
Cooke, G.A., *A Text-book of North Semitic Inscriptions*, Oxford University Press 1903
Cowley, A., *Aramaic Papyri of the Fifth Century B.C.*, Oxford University Press 1923
Cripps, R.S., *A Critical and Exegetical Commentary on the Book of Amos*, 2nd ed., SPCK 1955
Danby, H., *The Mishnah, Translated from the Hebrew with introduction and brief explanatory notes*, Oxford University Press 1933
Dead Sea Scrolls of St Mark's Monastery, The, ed. M. Burrows, 2 vols., New Haven, Conn., 1950-51
Discoveries in the Judaean Desert, edd. D. Barthélemy, R. de Vaux and others, 5 vols., Oxford University Press 1955-1968
Donner, H., and Röllig, W., edd., *Kanaanäische und Aramäische Inschriften*, 3 vols., Wiesbaden 1962
Driver, G.R., *Aramaic Documents of the Fifth Century B.C.*, Oxford University Press 1954
– *Canaanite Myths and Legends*, T. and T. Clark 1956
Driver, S.R., *An Introduction to the Literature of the Old Testament*, 7th

ed., T. and T. Clark 1898
– *Notes on the Hebrew Text and Topography of the Books of Samuel*, Oxford University Press 1913
– and Gray, G.B., *A Critical and Exegetical Commentary on the Book of Job* (ICC), 1921
Eichrodt, W., *Theology of the Old Testament* (OTL) 2 vols., 1961, 1967 (*Theologie des Alten Testaments*, Göttingen 1959, 1964)
Eissfeldt, O., *The Old Testament. An Introduction*, Blackwell 1966 (*Einleitung in das Alte Testament*, 3rd ed., Tübingen 1964)
Field, F., ed., *Origenis Hexaplorum quae supersunt*, 2 vols., Oxford 1875
Genesis Apocryphon, The, edd. N. Avigad and Y. Yadin, Jerusalem 1956
Gray, G.B., *A Critical and Exegetical Commentary on the Book of Isaiah*, I (Chapters I-XXVII) (ICC), 1912
Gröndahl, F., *Die Personennamen der Texts aus Ugarit*, Rome 1967
Gunkel, H., *Genesis übersetzt und erklärt*, 5th ed., Göttingen 1922
– *Einleitung in die Psalmen*, ed. J. Begrich, Göttingen 1933
Harper, W.R., *A Critical and Exegetical Commentary on Amos and Hosea* (ICC), 1905
Huffmon, H.B., *Amorite Personal Names in the Mari Texts. A Structural and Lexical Study*, Baltimore 1965
Kautzsch, E., ed., *Die Apokryphen und Pseudepigraphen des Alten Testaments*, 2 vols., Tübingen 1900
Knudtzon, J.A., *Die Amarna-Tafeln*, 2 vols., Leipzig 1915
Koch, K., *The Growth of the Biblical Tradition*, A. and C. Black 1969 (*Was ist Formgeschichte? Neue Wege der Bibelexegese*, Neukirchen-Vluyn 1965)
Kraeling, E.G., ed., *The Brooklyn Museum Aramaic Papyri*, 1953
Kraus, H.-J., *Psalmen* (BKAT 15), 1960
– *Threni* (BKAT 20), 1960
Lambert, W.G., *Babylonian Wisdom Literature*, Oxford University Press 1960
Luckenbill, D.D., *Ancient Records from Assyria and Babylon*, 2 vols., Chicago 1927
McKane, W., *Proverbs* (OTL), 1970
Mishna, ed. H. Albeck, 6 vols., Jerusalem 1952-57
Montgomery, J.A., and Gehman, H.S., *A Critical and Exegetical Commentary on the Books of Kings* (ICC), 1951
Moore, G.A., *A Critical and Exegetical Commentary on Judges* (ICC), 1895
Mowinckel, S., *The Psalms in Israel's Worship*, 2 vols., Blackwell 1962 (*Offersang og Sangoffer*, Oslo 1951)
New Testament in Syriac, The, British and Foreign Bible Society 1919
North, C.R., *The Second Isaiah. Introduction, Translation and Commentary to Chapters XL-LV*, Clarendon Press 1964
Noth, M., *Die israelitische Personennamen*, Stuttgart 1928
– *Exodus* (OTL) 1962 (*Das zweite Buch Mose. Exodus, ATD* 5, 1959)
– *Leviticus* (OTL) 1965 (*Das dritte Buch Mose. Leviticus*, ATD 6, 1962)
– *Das Buch Josua* (ATD 9), 2nd ed., 1953

Porteous, N.W., *Daniel. A Commentary* (OTL) 1965 (*Das Danielbuch*, ATD 23, 1962)
Pritchard, J., ed., *Ancient Near Eastern Texts relating to the Old Testament*, 2nd ed. Princeton 1955
– *The Ancient Near East. Supplementary Texts and Pictures relating to the Old Testament*, Princeton 1969
Quran, The, ed. G. Flügel, Leipzig 1834
Rabin, C., *The Zadokite Documents*, Clarendon Press 1958
Rad, G. von, *Genesis* (OTL), 1961 (*Das erste Buch Mose, Genesis*, ATD 2-4, 1956)
– *Old Testament Theology*, 2 vols., Oliver and Boyd 1962-65 (*Theologie des Alten Testaments*, Munich 1957-60)
– *Deuteronomy* (OTL), 1966 (*Das fünfte Buch Mose. Deuteronomium*, ATD 8, 1964)
Robinson, T.H., and Horst, F., *Die zwölf kleine Propheten* (HAT 14), 3rd ed., 1964
Rossini, K.C., *Chrestomathia Arabica Meridionalis Epigraphica*, Rome 1931
Rudolph, W., *Esra und Nehemia* (HAT 20), 1949
– *Chronikbücher*, (HAT 21), 1955
– *Jeremia* (HAT 12), 1958
Ryckmans, G., *Les Noms Propres Sud-Sémitiques*, 3 vols., Louvain 1934-5
Segert, S., 'Die Sprache der moabitischen Königsinschrift', *Archiv Orientální* 29, 1961, pp.197-268
Septuaginta, ed. A. Rahlfs, Stuttgart 1933
Singer, S., ed., *A Critical and Exegetical Commentary on Genesis* (ICC), 2nd ed., 1930
Stenning, J., ed., *The Targum of Isaiah*, Clarendon Press 1949
Talmud Babli, Jerusalem (printed Wilna) 1930
Talmud Yerushalmi, Jerusalem (printed Venice) 1930
Tosephta, ed. M.S. Zuckermandel, Trier 1877, reprinted Jerusalem 1963
Weiser, A., *Introduction to the Old Testament*, Darton, Longman and Todd 1961 (*Einleitung in das Alte Testament*, 4th ed., Göttingen 1957)
– *The Psalms* (OTL), 1962 (*Die Psalmen*, ATD 14/15, 5th ed., 1959)
Westermann, C., *Isaiah 40-66* (OTL) 1969 (*Das Buch Jesaia, Kapitel 40-66*, ATD 19, 1966)
Wolff, H.W., *Dodekapropheten, I. Hosea* (BKAT 14/1), 1961
Würthwein, E., *The Text of the Old Testament*, Blackwell 1957 (*Der Text des Alten Testament*, Stuttgart 1952)
Yadin, Y., ed., *The Scroll of the War of the Sons of Light against the Sons of Darkness*, (trans. B. and C. Rabin), Oxford University Press 1962
Zimmerli, W., *Ezechiel* (BKAT 13), 1969

3. *Grammars, Dictionaries, and Concordances*

Aistleitner, J., *Wörterbuch der ugaritischen Sprache*, 3rd ed., Berlin 1967

Bauer, H., and Leander, P., *Historische Grammatik der Hebräischen Sprache des Alten Testaments*, Halle 1922

Beeston, A.F.L., *A Descriptive Grammar of Epigraphic South Arabian*, London 1962

Bergsträsser, G., *Einführung in die semitischen Sprachen*, Munich 1928

Bezold, C., *Babylonisch-Assyrisches Glossar*, Heidelberg 1926

Brockelmann, C., *Grundriss der vergleichenden Grammatik der semitischen Sprachen*, 2 vols., Berlin 1908-13

– *Lexicon Syriacum*, 2nd ed., Halle 1928

Brown, F., Driver, S.R., and Briggs, C.A., *Hebrew and English Lexicon of the Old Testament*, Oxford 1907

Cantineau, G., *Le Nabatéen*, 2 vols., Paris 1930-32

Castellus, E., *Lexicon Heptaglotton*, London 1669

Chicago Assyrian Dictionary, ed. A.L. Oppenheim and others, 1956

Cohen, D., and Zafrani, H., *Grammaire de l'hébreu vivant*, Paris 1968

Dalman, G., *Grammatik des jüdisch-palästinischen Aramäisch*, 1905

Deimel, A., *Sumerisches Lexicon*, 4 vols., Rome 1928-50

Dillmann, A., *Lexicon Linguae Aethiopicae*, Leipzig 1865

– *Ethiopic Grammar*, London 1907

Epstein, J.N., *Diqduq ᵃramit bablit (Grammar of Babylonian Aramaic)*, Jerusalem 1960

Erman, A., and Grapow, H., *Wörterbuch der ägyptischen Sprache*, 5 vols., Leipzig 1926-31

Freytag, G.W., *Lexicon Arabico-Latinum*, Halle 1930

Friedrich, J., *Phönizisch-punische Grammatik*, Rome 1951

Gardiner, A., *Egyptian Grammar. An Introduction to the Study of Hieroglyphs*, 3rd ed., Oxford University Press 1957

Gelb, I.J., 'La lingua degli amoriti', *Atti della Accademia nazionale dei Lincei*, VIII, 1958 (Rendiconti della classe di scienze morali, storiche e filologiche, 13), pp.143-64

Gesenius' Hebrew Grammar, ed. E. Kautzsch, 2nd English ed. by A.E. Cowley, Oxford 1910

Gordon, C.H., *Ugaritic Textbook* (Analecta Orientalia 38), Rome 1965

Hatch, E., and Redpath, H.A., *A Concordance to the Septuagint*, Oxford 1897

Jastrow, M., *A Dictionary of the Targumim, the Talmud Babli and Yerushalmi, and the Midrashic Literature*, 2 vols., London 1903

Jean, C.-F., and Hoftijzer, J., *Dictionnaire des inscriptions sémitiques de l'ouest*, Leiden 1965

Joüon, P., *Grammaire de l'hébreu biblique*, Rome 1947

Koehler, L., and Baumgartner, W., *Lexicon in Veteris Testamenti Libros*, Leiden 1953; *Supplementum*, 1958

Kuhn, K.G., *Konkordanz zu den Qumran-Texten*, Göttingen 1960

Lane, E.W., *Arabic-English Lexicon*, 8 vols., London 1863-93

Levy, J., *Neuhebräisches und chaldäisches Wörterbuch über die Talmudim und Midraschim*, 4 vols., Leipzig 1876-89

Mandelkern, S., *Veteris Testamenti Concordantiae Hebraicae atque Chaldaicae*, rev. ed., Tel Aviv 1962

Megiddo Modern Dictionary, The, Hebrew-English, edd. R. Sivan and E.A. Levenston, 2nd ed., Tel Aviv 1967

Mercier, G., *Vocabulaires et textes berbères dans le dialecte berbère des ʿAit Izdeg*, Rabat 1937

Moscati, S., ed., *An Introduction to the Comparative Grammar of the Semitic Languages. Phonology and Morphology*, Wiesbaden 1964

Muss-Arnold, W., *A Concise Dictionary of the Assyrian Language. Assyrisch-Englisch-Deutsches Handwörterbuch*, 2 vols., Berlin 1894-1905

Neubauer, A., ed., *Book of Hebrew Roots by Marwan b. Janah*, Oxford 1875

Nöldeke, Th., *Kurzgefasste syrische Grammatik*, 2nd ed., Leipzig 1898

Payne Smith, R., *Thesaurus Syriacus*, 2 vols., Oxford 1868-97

Petermann, J.H., *Brevis linguae Samaritanae grammatica, litteratura, chrestomathia, cum glossario*, Berlin 1873

Rabin, C., *ye sodot ha-diqduq ha-mašwe šel ha-lašon ha-ʿibrit (Elements of the Comparative Grammar of the Hebrew Language)*, Hebrew University, Jerusalem 1965

Rosén, H.B., *ha-ʿibrit še-lanu (Our Hebrew)*, Tel Aviv 1956

— *A Textbook of Israeli Hebrew, with an Introduction to the Classical Language*, Chicago 1962

Rosenthal, F., *A Grammar of Biblical Aramaic*, Wiesbaden 1961

Scharfstein, Z., *ʾọsar hammillim w^e hanniwim (Thesaurus of Words and Phrases)*, 3rd ed., Tel Aviv 1964

Schultens, A., *Origines Hebraeae sive Hebraicae Linguae antiquissima natura et indoles ex Arabiae penetralibus revocata*, Leiden 1761

Schulthess, F., *Lexicon Syropalaestinum*, Berlin 1903

Segal, M.H., *A Grammar of Mishnaic Hebrew*, 2nd ed., Oxford 1958

Stevenson, W.B., *Grammar of Palestinian Jewish Aramaic*, 2nd ed., Oxford 1962

Soden, W.von, *Grundriss der akkadischen Grammatik* (Analecta Orientalia 33), Rome 1952

— *Akkadisches Handwörterbuch*, Wiesbaden 1959ff.

Ungnad, A., *Babylonisch-Assyrische Grammatik*, Munich 1906

Wagner, M., *Die lexikalische und grammatikalische Aramäismen in alttestamentlichen Hebräisch* (BZAW 96), 1966

Wehr, H., *A Dictionary of Modern Written Arabic*, ed. J.M. Cowan, Wiesbaden 1961

Wright, W., *A Grammar of the Arabic Language*, 3rd ed., Cambridge University Press 1896-8.

Zorell, F., *Lexicon Hebraicum et Aramaicum Veteris Testamenti*, Rome 1940ff.

Index of Hebrew words

Index of Biblical passages

Index of Persons and Subjects